# THE TABERNACLE TOUR

Joe Olivio

Copyright © 2007 by Joe Olivio

*Tabernacle Tour*
by Joe Olivio

Printed in the United States of America

ISBN 978-1-60266-993-2

All rights reserved solely by the author. The author guarantees all contents are original and do not infringe upon the legal rights of any other person or work. No part of this book may be reproduced in any form without the permission of the author. The views expressed in this book are not necessarily those of the publisher.

Unless otherwise indicated, Bible quotations are taken from KJV. Copyright © 2001 by Thomas Nelson.

www.xulonpress.com

Table of contents                         Page

Introduction ............................  1
1. Gate................................... 18
2. Brazen Altar.......................... 25
3. Laver.................................. 44
4. Curtain Door.......................... 51
5. Table of Shewbread................... 61
6. Golden Altar.......................... 70
7. Candlestick........................... 78
8. Veil................................... 92
9. Ark ................................... 100
10. Mercy Seat, Cherubim............... 108
11. Tabernacle Proper................... 116
12. Pillar of Cloud and Fire............ 128
13. Day of Atonement................... 134
14. Jesus, Perfect Lamb of God........ 163
15. Typology chart .................... 174

# THE TABERNACLE
### God's Plan of Redemption through Jesus Christ
### the Perfect Tabernacle   Heb.9:11

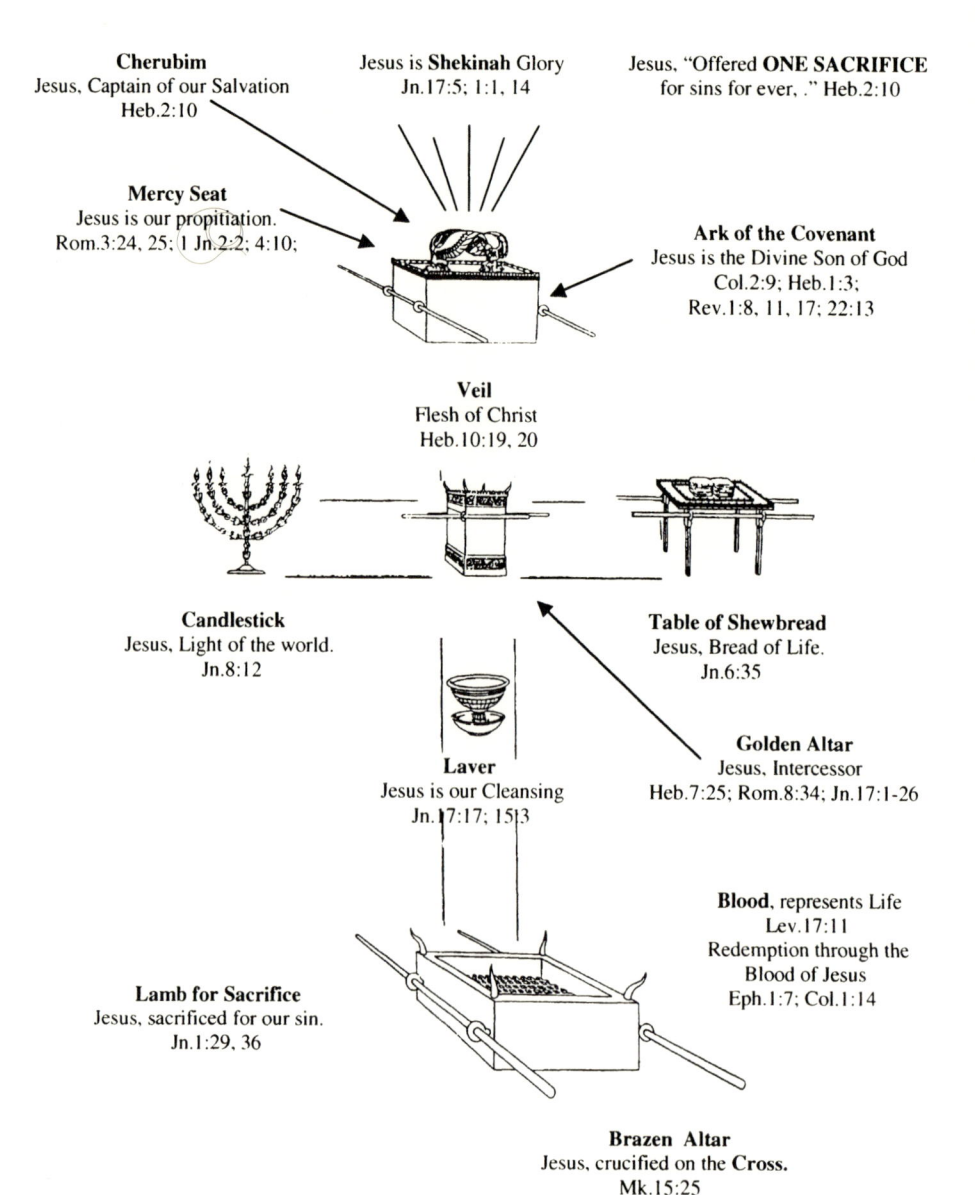

**Cherubim**
Jesus, Captain of our Salvation
Heb.2:10

Jesus is **Shekinah** Glory
Jn.17:5; 1:1, 14

Jesus, "Offered **ONE SACRIFICE** for sins for ever, ." Heb.2:10

**Mercy Seat**
Jesus is our propitiation.
Rom.3:24, 25; 1 Jn.2:2; 4:10;

**Ark of the Covenant**
Jesus is the Divine Son of God
Col.2:9; Heb.1:3;
Rev.1:8, 11, 17; 22:13

**Veil**
Flesh of Christ
Heb.10:19, 20

**Candlestick**
Jesus, Light of the world.
Jn.8:12

**Table of Shewbread**
Jesus, Bread of Life.
Jn.6:35

**Golden Altar**
Jesus, Intercessor
Heb.7:25; Rom.8:34; Jn.17:1-26

**Laver**
Jesus is our Cleansing
Jn.17:17; 15:3

**Blood**, represents Life
Lev.17:11
Redemption through the
Blood of Jesus
Eph.1:7; Col.1:14

**Lamb for Sacrifice**
Jesus, sacrificed for our sin.
Jn.1:29, 36

**Brazen Altar**
Jesus, crucified on the **Cross**.
Mk.15:25

# THE TABERNACLE   Exodus chapters 25-40

**Introduction**:
When God delivered the nation of Israel from Egyptian bondage. While they were in route to the Promise Land He gave them a Tabernacle in which to serve Him. Ex.25:8
Moses walked into the Cloud of Glory on Mount Sinai. God showed him a pattern of the Tabernacle in heaven from which he made the earthy Tabernacle. Ex.24:15-18

Moses made the Tabernacle exactly as God showed him in the mount, because every color, metal, numeral and piece of furniture contained therein is a type of His complete plan of redemption that was fulfilled in Jesus Christ, before it came to pass! Ex.25:40

**God teaches His Great Spiritual Truths of Redemption by using types**.
Jesus established the typology of His Tabernacle.
In Jn.1:45 Philip finds Nathanel and said, "We have found Him, of whom Moses in the Law, and the prophets did write, Jesus of Nazareth, the Son of Joseph." Deut.18:18; Mt.2:23

In chapter 5, verse 46, Jesus said, "Had you believed Moses, you would have believed Me. Moses wrote of Me."
In Lk.24:27 After His Resurrection, Jesus appeared to His disciples. "Beginning at Moses and all the prophets, He expounded unto them in all the Scriptures the things concerning Himself."
In verse 44 He said, "These are the words which I spoke unto you, while I was yet with you, that all things must be fulfilled, which were written in the Law of Moses, in the prophets, and in the Psalms, concerning Me.
In verse 45 "Then Jesus opened their understanding that they might understand the Scriptures." Deut.18:15; Jere.23:5; Ac.3:22,23; 13:23

## Principles of Typology

- ology means the study of something. A branch of learning. A type is the study of a person, place or thing in the Bible which God designed to illustrate and show ahead of its time. An event that will appear in the future. A type is shown in the Old Testament and appears in the New Testament.
Typology is the study of types.

The Tabernacle in the wilderness is a type of Jesus Christ. We will use the lamb for our definitions of a type.

Many Scriptures give us an explanation of a type. Our first definition of a type is found in
1 Cor.10:11
"Now all these things happened unto them for examples: and they are written for our admonition upon whom the ends of the world are come."

The Bible defines a type:
1. As an **example**. An example is something chosen to show what another thing is like. A type is an example of what is to come. The Tabernacle is called an example and shows us the complete plan of redemption that we have already received in Jesus Christ before God brought it to pass.

Example:
The lamb upon the altar of sacrifice for sin was only an example of God's true Lamb, the Lord Jesus Christ.

2. **As a Shadow**. Heb.8:4,5
A shadow reflects substance. The Tabernacle is called a shadow and was only a reflection of the great plan of redemption fulfilled in Jesus Christ. Heb.10:1 A shadow of heavenly things.
A shadow of good things to come.
Example:

The lamb for sacrifice for sin was only a shadow of our redeemer the Lord, Jesus Christ.

3. As a **Figure**. Heb.9:8,9
   A figure is an outline or sketch of something. The Tabernacle is called a figure and is only an outline or sketch of the great plan of redemption fulfilled in Jesus Christ.
   Heb.9:24 Only a figure of the true.
Example:
The lamb upon the altar of sacrifice for sin was only a figure of the Messiah.

4. As a **Pattern**. Heb.8:5; Ex.25:9; 26:30
A pattern is a plan used as a guide in making something. The Tabernacle is called a pattern. A plan to lead and guide us to the fulfillment of God's great and perfect redemption in Jesus Christ. Heb.9:23 The pattern of things in the heavens.
Example:
The lamb upon the altar of sacrifice for sin was only a pattern of Jesus Christ, our Eternal Life.

5. The Tabernacle is called a **Witness**. Num.17:7
   To detail the complete plan of Redemption in Jesus Christ. Ac.7:44
A witness is a person who saw or heard an event and can give a firsthand account of that event. The Tabernacle is a witness to Jesus Christ in redemption, before His Coming in the flesh. It was an object of witness.
Example:
The lamb upon the altar of sacrifice for sin was only a witness of the true and faithful witness the Lord Jesus Christ. Rev.1:5; 3:14

6. God called the Tabernacle by **Appointment**. Ac.7:44
   An appointment is to set a date, day, time and place to

examine, show or to explain a certain thing. The Tabernacle was an appointment under the Law to direct Israel to the Spiritual Realities in Christ their Messiah. The Law was our schoolmaster. It led us to Christ. Gal.3:24,25

Jesus did not destroy the Law. He fulfilled the Law. Mt.5:17

We are not under the Law, but under Grace. Justified by faith. The Law could not make the comers perfect, but the Precious Blood of Jesus Christ can. Gal.2:16; Heb.7:19

We are justified and have mercy through faith in His Blood. Rom.3:25

"Whom God hath set forth to be a Propitiation through faith in His Blood, to declare His righteousness for the remission of sins that are past, through the forbearance of God."

Example:
The lamb upon the altar of sacrifice for sin was only a type of the true appointment of the Lord Jesus Christ in the time of Grace.

7. God orders Moses to make the Tabernacle after the Fashion he had seen in the mount. Ac.7:44
   A fashion is to make, form and shape a thing. The Tabernacle was the house, tent or outer covering of Jesus Christ the Perfect Tabernacle in type. Heb.9:11
   It was made after the fashion of God. Jesus is God's fashion. The very image of God. The flesh of Jesus was the veil of the Godhead. Col.1:15; Jn.14:9

Example:
The lamb upon the altar of sacrifice for sin was only a fashion of our Lord Jesus Christ. The True fashion of God. Moses did not see the Grand Tabernacle in heaven. He saw a copy of it

when he walked into the Cloud of Glory.

The Cloud of Glory is a type of the Holy Spirit that dwells in us. We have the Perfect Tabernacle in our Living Lamb, the Lord Jesus Christ.

What the Bible says, not only about the Tabernacle, but about all the Old Testament Scripture is:
"Whatsoever things were written aforetime were written for our learning, that we through patience and comfort of the Scripture might have hope." Rom.15:4

**Reasons why we should study the Typology of the Tabernacle**:
In the Tabernacle are Spiritual Realities that are only revealed in the resurrected all-powerful Christ.

The truth of redemption comes alive with new and deeper meaning. The hard to understand Scriptures are made very clear. Simple and easy to understand

It shows us ahead of time the Person, work and service of our Lord, Jesus Christ in Redemption. So, we would know Him when in the fullness of time He came to redeem us from sin by the sacrifice of Himself. Gal.4:4

God gave it to us as a teaching tool for our study in redemption. Eph. 3:3; Heb.10:22.

It is a complete object lesson. A picture. A show and tell in redemption. It pointed Israel to Christ and it points us to Christ as we look back in a continual learning process in redemption.

The typology of the Tabernacle is a pure revelation in grace! The "Mystery of Redemption" revealed.

We cannot understand the true wonders of the Bible in the New Testament without an understanding of the Tabernacle and its Typology. Especially the epistle to the Hebrews. The Bible interprets itself. The New Testament is in the Old concealed. The Old Testament is in the New revealed.

**Why Israel went into Egypt.**
God prophesied to Abraham that the children of Israel would be in Egyptian bondage 430 years. Gen.15:14-16. Ex.12:40

He promised to bless the world through Abraham's seed.
Gen.12:3; 18:18; 22:17,18; 26:4; Deut.1:10; Ac.3:25
This blessing would extend through Christ to all generations and people of the world. Gal.3:16; Ac.3:26
The message of redemption is found in the book of Exodus which is called the book of redemption in the Old Testament.

When the nation of Israel came into Egypt they were very few in number. About 70 souls. Gen.46:27; Ex.1:5; Deut.10:22; Ac.7:14. In a short time they multiplied to upwards of 603,550 men over 20 years of age. In addition to women and children. (about 2 ½ million. Ex.38:26 God had literally fulfilled His promise.

After having governed Egypt for 80 years, Joseph was now dead. The important services preformed by Him were forgotten by all of the Egyptians. Gen.50:26; Ex.1:6; Ac.7:15

A new king arose over Egypt who did not know of Joseph. Ex.1:8; Ac.7:18,19. Having great pride in himself he disapproved of the system of government which Joseph had established.
Through his quick high rise to pride and power this jealous, cruel king deceived the Israelites and then led them into captivity and slavery. The devil still uses these same tactics today! He tries to deceive us and then lead us into the captivity of sin.

In Egypt Pharaoh appointed taskmasters over Israel to afflict them. Ex.1:11 These masters of burdens drove the Israelites to build treasure cities for Pharaoh. He assigned them hard and wearing toils to break down their physical strength. To crush their spirit. To destroy their hope for liberty and to shut down their desire to worship and serve God. Ex.3:7; 5:6-14

God heard the cries of His people in Egypt. It was 430 years the children of Israel were held in slavery and bondage under the hand of Pharaoh. On the self same day of His prophecy to Abraham God called Moses from the burning bush on Mt Horeb to be the deliverer of His people. Moses is a type of Christ the True Deliverer.
Ex.12:40,41; Deut.18:15-18; Ac.3:20-22; 7:6,7; Gal.3:17

**The Great Exodus began**.
**Exodus**, means a mass departure. God called His people to make the Great Exodus and to serve Him. To leave the world, the flesh and the devil behind. The children of Israel left it all behind.

Pharaoh's heart was hardened. He resisted, but through the ten plagues God put upon Egypt. Pharaoh let God's people go free.

Ex.7:14 – chapter 11
These plagues were very well chosen by God Almighty to show the Egyptians that their ten false deities were helpless against God's power. God destroyed all the faith of the Egyptian people in their false gods. Many of the Egyptians made the Exodus with the nation of Israel. It was a mixed multitude.
Ex.12:38; Num.11:4

**Out of Egypt**, (Receive Christ! Come out from among the world, and serve the Living God)!
The Great Exodus of the Israelites from Egypt is a lesson in type. Just as Israel was called to leave Egypt with all of its false gods,

we are called to come out from among this present evil world with its false gods to serve the Living God!

**Pharaoh**, is a type of Satan. A ruler of the world. God delivered the people out from under his hand.

**Egyptian Taskmasters**, are a type of binders and oppressors that kept Israel from the worship, will and service of God. He freed them from all of these oppressors. Ac.10:38

**Egypt**, is a type of sin and the world. A place of death and bondage. God called them out from that present evil world. Gal.1:4

To understand God's teaching tool (the typology of His Tabernacle in Redemption) we must apply it to our lives and live it!

**We are a type of spiritual Israel**. Rom.4: 11,16; Gal.3:29; 6:16.
By the Holy Spirit of God in Christ, we have been called out from under Satan's hand. Out from under his control. We have been freed from all the hindrances that keep us from the worship, will and service of God. We have been called out from sin, slavery, bondage and the captivity of this present evil world to make the Great Exodus to worship and serve the Living God!

Jesus said, "Get thee hence, Satan: for it is written, thou shalt worship the Lord thy God, and Him only shalt thou serve." Mt.4:10; Lk.4:8
We have come out from among this present evil world.
We have left it all gladly!
2 Cor.6:17, 18; 7:1; Rom.12:1,2; Rev.18:4; Isa.52:11.

**The nation of Israel left Egypt with great riches and wealth**.
Just prior to Israel leaving the bondage and slavery of the Egyptian taskmasters God commanded them to ask for gold, silver and clothes from their heathen neighbors.

Because of the horrible plagues God put upon Egypt, these Egyptians were gripped with fear and horror. They were more than happy to be rid of these people at last. They gave to those who departed all that they desired. Gen.15:14-16. Ex.3:22; 11:2;12:36.

**The Calling, Building and Setting up of the Tabernacle.** Ex.25:40
God called His people out of Egypt. The Passover marked the beginning of their 40 year journey through the wilderness in route to the Promise Land.

First, God's people were redeemed by the blood of the Passover Lamb and then the Cloud of Glory came to lead them.

We have been saved through the Blood of Jesus Christ and then led out of the world by the power of the Holy Spirit!

The children of Israel were to reach the Promise Land in forty days, but because of their sin the Lord said it would take them forty years. Num.14:33,34.
They were taken through forty years of wilderness to purge out carnality. To crucify their fleshly nature to find out if they would be faithful to God.
Rom. 6:6,7; 18:1; 1Cor.3:1-3; Gal. 2:20; 5:24.

The wilderness journey speaks to us of that great buffer zone between the world and the Promise Land for the trying of our faith!

The nation of Israel reached Mt. Sinai and camped in the wilderness. Ex.19:1
Moses ascended the Mount. God gave him a pattern of the Tabernacle to erect on earth.

In this forty year journey the children of Israel were given a Tabernacle in which to serve God. He calls the Tabernacle **The Church in the wilderness**. Ac.7:38

The Tabernacle was made with the freewill offerings.
Ex.25:2; 35:5; 36:5-7
Moses called for the materials only from those persons who were willing to give from their hearts.
The people brought more than enough.

God was the Architect of the Tabernacle. He showed Moses a pattern of the Tabernacle in heaven. The Tabernacle of the Exodus was a copy of a copy of the Grand Tabernacle in heaven.

Moses was the master builder. He was commanded to make all the furniture. Divine wisdom was given to Bezaleel to make it. The skillful craftsmen were Bezaleel, Aholiab, wise hearted women and everyone that was willing helped do the work.
Ex.31:2-7; 35:21-33; 36:1,2

All of God's people have been called to serve and are of equal important to the service of God! Mk.13:34.

God tells us, Don't go down to Egypt (the world) for help! "I am the Lord your God, which brings you out from under the burdens of the Egyptians." Ex.6:6,7.
God has brought us out from the hand of Satan and burdens of this present evil world!

The Tabernacle was the Meeting Place between God and His people. Ex.25:22; 29:42,43,45;30:6; Num.17:4.
Jesus is our Meeting Place now in His Church. Heb.9:11.

Moses sprinkled the blood of the lamb upon God's Word and upon all the people. Ex. 24:8; Heb.9:19; Rev.1:5.
We were sprinkled, purified and washed in the Life giving Blood of Jesus Christ. Heb.13:12

The Tabernacle was Sanctified by the Glory of the Lord.
Ex. 29:43,44; 40:34; Num. 9:15.

Jesus is the Sanctified and Glorified One.
God's Holy, Living Word. Jn.10:36.
Jesus was Sanctified and sent into the world.
We need to be sanctified before we are sent into the world to witness. Jn.17:16,17; 1 Cor.1:2,30.

Jesus was filled with the Spirit. Lk.4:1.
We need to be filled with the Spirit.
Jn.17:17; Ac.2:4; 1:8; Eph. 5:17,18.
The evidence of our salvation is the indwelling of the Holy Spirit. He gives us a power filled life. Rom. 8:9-16.

The Tabernacle and the priests were sanctified and filled with the Glory of the Lord. Ex.29:43,44; 40:34; Num.9:15
The Tabernacle and vessels were sprinkled with blood.
Heb.9:21, 22
We have been sprinkled, purified and washed in the blood of our Lamb, Jesus Christ. Rev.1:5,6
It is the blood of Jesus that sanctifies us.

God called for the dedication of the Tabernacle when it was completed according to His pattern in every detail. Moses anointed it, and the Presence of God filled it.

The Tabernacle and all within were anointed and sanctified with Holy Oil. Ex.30:26; 40:9,11; Lev. 8:10,11; Num.7:1
Jesus is the Anointed One.
Isa.42:1; 61:1; Ac.10:38; Mt. 12:18-21;3:16,17; Lk.4:18,19.

The Cloud of Glory appeared above and upon it.
Ex. 24:17,18; 40:34; Num.9:15-23

The Tabernacle was a movable tent suited to the unsettled condition of Israel as they journeyed from Egypt to the Promise Land. 2 Sam.7:6,7.
Jesus the Perfect Tabernacle dwells in us and we in Him in our unsettled condition on this earth's journey to our true home in heaven. Heb.11:13

**Pillar of Cloud and Fire**.
The Cloud of Glory, is a type of the Holy Spirit. the Pillar of Fire, is a symbol of the Presence of God.

God led His people with the Cloud and Pillar of Fire through the wilderness on their way to the Promise Land as He leads us through this world to our home in heaven today in Jesus by the power His Holy Spirit. Rom.8:14; Gal.5:18

The Cloud of Glory protected and led Israel by day and night during their abode in the wilderness as long as they kept God's commandments. Ex.14:29,20; 40:38; Num.9:15,16
God protects us from our enemies and separates us from the world as long as we obey His Holy Spirit and keep His Word.

In this "Time of Grace" God speaks to us through His Son. Heb.1:2. The Old Way of worship was superseded by Christ's death when "The Veil of the temple was rent in twain from the top to the bottom." Mt.27:51; Mk.15:38; Lk.23:45; Jn.2:19-22

Now our redemption points to the Living God as revealed in Jesus Christ. We may enter into the presence of God now through the Blood of Jesus. Heb.10:19, 20; 6:19, 20

Moses saw God's Glory.  We have His Glory now in Christ! When God dwelt in the Tabernacle of old among the Jews only the priests saw His Glory.  When Jesus dwelt in the flesh among men His disciples saw His Glory manifested in His gracious words, miraculous acts, signs, wonders and miracles.

In Lk.4:18,19 Jesus said,
"The Spirit of the Lord is upon me, because He hath anointed Me to preach the gospel to the poor; He hath sent me to heal the brokenhearted, to preach deliverance to the captives, and recovering of sight to the blind, to set at liberty them that are bruised, To preach the acceptable year of the Lord."
Isa.61,2

The Tabernacle was designed for the manifestation of God's Presence and for the worship of Him. Ex.25:8; 29:42,43
The Church today is designed for the manifestation of God's Presence. The worship of Him and for the Glory in Christ by the power of the Holy Spirit.

The death of Jesus gives us salvation.
His resurrection gives us eternal life.
His ascension gives us power to live above this present evil world, because He has given us His Holy Spirit.

The Cloud of Glory, is a type of the Holy Spirit within us.
The Pillar of Fire, is a type of the Holy Spirit upon us.

We are filled with grace and truth teaching the way to the kingdom of God.  We have the fullest proof of His divinity because He dwells in us. In performing miracles, healings with unending answered prayer in the name of Jesus. In the full power of His Spirit! God calls everyone who will hear His voice to be a separated and redeemed people.  Nothing can stop the Exodus!

Let's examine God's way of calling a separated people unto Himself through Jesus Christ the Perfect Tabernacle.
Ex.33:16; Lev. 20:24,26; Num.23:9; Deut.33:28.
2 Cor.6:2,17; Isa.1:18; Rev.18:4; Gal.1:4; 6:14; 1 Jn.2:15-17;


**"Let them make Me a Sanctuary** (Tabernacle)
**that I may dwell among them."**
Ex.25:8,22; 29:45,46

The earthly Tabernacle, recorded in Exodus means, God dwelling with His people is a type of Jesus Christ who is a greater and more Perfect Tabernacle, not made with hands.
Heb.9:11; Col.2:9

It is a type of Christ and His Church of which He is the head. Col.1:18
A type of the believer. 2 or.5:1; 2 Pet.1:13; Heb.3:6
All born again believers are His Church. Jn.3:3-7; 1:12,13

---

The Hebrew measure of a cubit is from the tip of the middle finger to the elbow which is 18 ins. This is the generally accepted measure of a cubit. This is the measurement we are using in the Bible study. The actual measure of a cubit whatever it may be does not affect the types in any way, shape or form.

# Outer Court

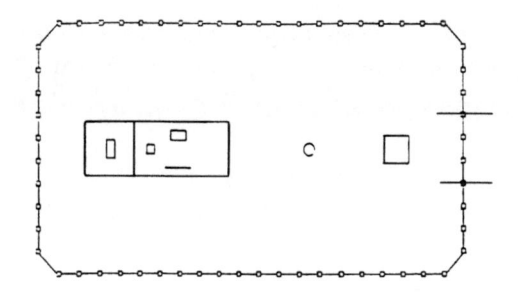

### Location.
The Outer Court was located in the Center of the nation of Israel. The twelve tribes were camped around the Court, speaks of Jesus the very Heart of God in the Center of our lives!

### Purpose.
The Outer Court was the Meeting Place for the people and the priests. Ex. 29:42,43
The linen fence was too high to see over and too low to see under. There was only one way into the Outer Court and that was through the Gate!
Jesus is the only way to come into the presence of God. Jn.14:6; Jn.3:3-5

### Physical Characteristics of the Outer Court.
Ex. 27:9-20; 38:9-20
The hangings of the Outer Court were made of fine twined linen. 150 ft. long on the south and north sides, by 75 ft. wide on the east and west ends. The white fine twined linen curtain hangings that made up the wall of the Court were suspended from sixty posts in sockets of brass.

Fine Twined Linen, speaks of the believers in Practical Righteousness. Rev.19:8, 14.

Our righteousness in Christ within. Phil.3:9

> "... not having mine own righteousness, which is of the law, but that which is through the faith of Christ, the righteousness which is of God by faith: Phil.3:9

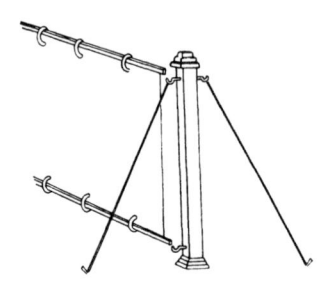

Gate Post

There were 20 posts on the south side and 20 on the north side. There were ten posts on the west end and ten on the east end with no corner posts. There was a 7 ½ spacing between each posts. From one side of the Gate around the Court to the other side of the Gate was 420 ft. All the posts were 7 ½ ft. high. The sockets of the Outer Court formed the foundation for the posts.

Fifty six posts for the Outer Court and four post for the Gate, equal sixty posts in all. **Posts**, speak of believers.

The posts tied upright with the heavy linen hangings between them, speak of our own weight while at the same time bearing the weight of others who are under His Redeeming Blood! We bear one another's burdens. Gal. 6:2,5; Ps.55:22.

The 4 Gate posts, speak of the 4 evangelist of the 4 gospels who proclaim the Glad Tidings of the salvation message of Jesus Christ.

**Border**, speaks of Safety. The Outer Court served as a barrier. It kept out the unbeliever. It received only the believer. It enclosed those who came to God with a sacrifice to receive forgiveness from their sins at the Brazen Altar.

To be inside the Outer Court was protection from spiritual death. It meant no separation from God. It was a border of safety.

We are protected from spiritual death and the evils of this world. We have come to Christ. Are under His precious blood.
Safe within the border of Salvation.

———————————

# Chapter 1

**The Gate, was the entrance into the Outer Court, where forgiveness from sin could be received:**

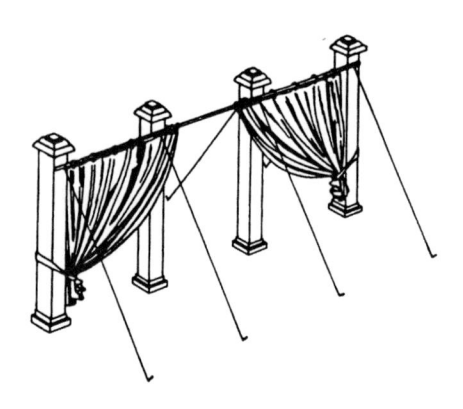

**Jesus said, "I am the way, the truth, and the life: no man can come unto the Father, but by Me." Jn.14:6**

Bible study outline No.1
1. **Visual illustration**
   Gate. Ex.27:16; 38:18,19
2. **Type of Christ**. Jesus is the Way.
   Mt.7:13,14; Lk.13:24-30; Ac.4:10-12
3. Applied to the believer.
   Repent. Mk1:15; Ac.2:38; 3:19;17:30; 20:21
4. **Believer's responsibility**.
   Confess Jesus before men. Rom.10:9,10

   It was called:
   Gate. Ex.27:16
   Curtain for the Door of the Court. Num. 3:26
   Door of the Court. Num.3:26

**Physical Characteristics** Ex.27:16; 38:18,19.
The dimensions of the Gate were 30 ft. wide with a (22 ½ ft. spacing on each side of the Gate. The Gate was located directly in the center of the Outer Court on the East end. The height was 7 ½ ft. The same height as the Court. There were 4 posts that made up the Gate identical to the other posts of the Court. The hangings of the Gate were made of fine twined linen wrought with needlework of blue, purple and scarlet.

**Typical Colors**, of the Gate and its hangings.
 **White**, speaks of His:
Righteousness.
2 Cor.5:21. Jesus was made, "Sin for us who knew no sin; that we might be made the righteousness of God in Him."

**Blue**, speaks of His Heavenly Nature.
   "Is the Lord from heaven." 1 Cor.15:47 Jn.6:38,33; 3:13;
    Eph. 4:9,10; Heb.4:14; Heb.9:2; 1 Tim.3:16
Jesus came from heaven, for more than 33 years. He was on this earth. His Heart and Mind was in heaven. He was heaven bound. Jesus returned to heaven. Jn.1:18, 3:13
We dwell in Him! Jn.14:20; 15:4
We have His Heavenly Nature! He dwells in us!
Jesus is in our hearts and minds. We too are heaven bound!

**Purple**, speaks of His Royalty; Kingship.
Lk,23:38; Mk15:26; Mt.27:37
"A superscription also was written over Him in letters of
  Greek, and Latin, and Hebrew, This is Jesus the King of
  the Jews." Jn.19:14; 19:19
  1 Tim. 6:15. Jesus is, "The King of kings, and Lord of lords;"
  Rev.17:14;19:6,12,14,16; Dan.2:47; Mk. 15:17,18

**Purple** also speaks of High Birth.
  Mt.2:1,2 Jesus was born from above!
  Mic.5:2-Mt.2:6; Jn.3:3; Jn.1:12,13

Jesus the King of kings came to earth in a royal birth. A high birth. Jesus the King came from above, was born from above! We have received the royal birth. Jn.3:3; 1:12,13 The high birth. We have been born from above! Ex.19:5; 1 Pet. 2:7-9.

**Scarlet**, (red or crimson) speaks of His Sacrifice. Heb.9:26.
Jesus, "Appeared to put away sin by the sacrifice of Himself."
I Cor.5:7 "Christ our passover is sacrificed for us."
Heb.10:12 Jesus, "One Sacrifice for sins for ever,"
We have received His Sacrifice and therefore become living sacrifices unto Him!

Rom.12:1 "That ye present your bodies a living sacrifice, holy, acceptable unto God, which is reasonable service."
Heb.13:15; Eph. 5:2

**Scarlet** also speaks of Atonement. Rom.5:9. "Being now justified by His blood, we shall be saved from wrath through Him."
v.11 "We also joy in God through our Lord Jesus Christ, by whom we have now received the atonement."

**Size**
The Gate for which the nation of Israel was to enter in through to receive forgiveness from sin at the Brazen Altar was a narrow gate! The Outer Court was very small in comparison with the camp. Heb.13:13.

In the light of the whole epistle of Hebrews it indicates that the "camp" refers to the religious world. The Outer Court and Gate were small. The camp was large.

There were only a few of those from among the crowds that really entered the Gate. So it is today!
In Mt.7:14 Jesus said, "Strait is the gate, and narrow is the way,

which leads unto life, and few there be that find it."

He said, "Many be called, but few chosen."
Mt.20:16; 22:14; Rev.17:14.

God's "Flock" is a "Little One." Jesus said, "Fear not Little Flock; for it is your Father's good pleasure to give you the kingdom." Lk.12:32

The height of the Gate was the same as the Court. Too high to see over. Too low to see under. The only way in to the Court was through the Gate!

Jesus is the only way to receive forgiveness from sin. We must enter in through Him, the Strait Gate! Jesus is the way to salvation! Jn.14:6

He said, "Enter ye in at the strait gate: for wide is the gate, and broad is the way that leads to destruction, and many there be which go in thereat:" Jn.10:9; Mt.7:13

Jesus speaks here of the public and private ways mentioned by the Jewish lawyers. The public roads were allowed to be 24 ft. wide. The private ways only 6 ft. wide.

The strait gate is found in Mt.7:12 Jesus said, "All things whatsoever ye would that men should do to you, do ye even so to them:" Lk.6:31.

This alone is the Strait Gate in which Jesus is speaking. To the unsaved this is a very hard and difficult thing to do! If you are not saved seek God through Christ for salvation!
2 Cor.7:10.
"For godly sorrow works repentance to salvation,"

and In Mt.713 Jesus said, "Wide is the Gate" to hell and very broad is this spacious roomy place that leads forward into destruction
eternal misery! Those who will not repent are in the broad road to hell! How strange it is that people are unwilling to give up their sin and worldly interests to secure their salvation.

In Mt.7:14 He said, "Few there be that find the Strait Gate." Jesus signifies a wicket! A small opening in a large door or entrance. Mt.19:24; 10:25; Lk.18:25

People are wedded to their own passions and do what pleases themselves. They are determined to follow the imaginations of their own hearts. Gen. 6:5

There are: Few who find the way to heaven;
Fewer yet who abide any time in it;
Fewer still who walk in it; and
Fewest of all who persevere unto the end!

Sin makes the strait gate narrow! We live in a sinful world! In the "Last Days!" Isa.5:14 tells us that "Hell hath enlarged herself. Opened her mouth without measure:"

Many wish and desire, but they do not make an effort therefore, because they are not in earnest and sincere they shall not get in the Strait Gate!

Many people say, "We have no time now to be saved. There are others who say, "I'm young, I have time to be saved." God tells us in 2 Cor.6:2
"Behold, now is the day of salvation."

Enter in through the Strait Gate which is Jesus Christ! Let your salvation be first. The purpose of your whole life. Put Christ first then He will give you power over sin and power to live for Him!

Jesus said, "Enter in at the strait gate: for many, I say unto you will seek to enter in, and shall not be able." Lk.13:24.

God gives us the greatest encouragement through repentance, prayer and godly sorrow to enter in!

All who are not saved may come at the invitation of the Savior! Rev. 22:17
"Whosoever will, let him take the water of life freely." Rev. 21:6

Material
The hangings for the Gate were made of fine twined linen, speaks of Practical Righteousness.

**Location**
The Gate was located at the East end of the Outer Court. Ex.27:13-16; 38:13-15.

It faced East toward the rising of the sun. Num. 2:3
Jesus said,
  "As the lightning cometh out of the East, and shines even unto the west: so shall also the Coming of the Son of Man be." Mt.24:27; Mt.24:30; Rev.1:7

**Purpose**
The purpose was to receive all who entered in through the Gate with a sacrifice at the Brazen Altar to receive forgiveness from their sins.

We have been forgiven from our sins, washed in the Blood of the Living Lamb, Jesus Christ! He is our Sacrifice!
Jesus saved us from our sin!

Jn.1:12,13; 3:16-18, 36; 6:37, 40, 47; Ac. 4:12; 10:43; 2 Cor.6:2; Josh.24:15; 1 Kgs.18:21; Isa.1:18.

**Evidences of Salvation**
Love for the brethren. I John 3:16.
Witness of the Spirit. Rom. 8:16.
Guidance of the Spirit. Rom. 8:14.
Love of God shed in our hearts. Rom. 5:5.
Fruits of the Spirit in our life. Gal. 5:22,23.
Keeping Christ's Commandments.1 Jn.2:3-6.
Doing righteousness. 1 John 3:10.
Overcoming the world. 1 John 5:4.
Spiritual understanding.
   1 Jn.2:20, 27; Jn.5:20; 1 Cor.2:14, 15

# Chapter 2

## The Brazen Altar, speaks of Sacrifice.

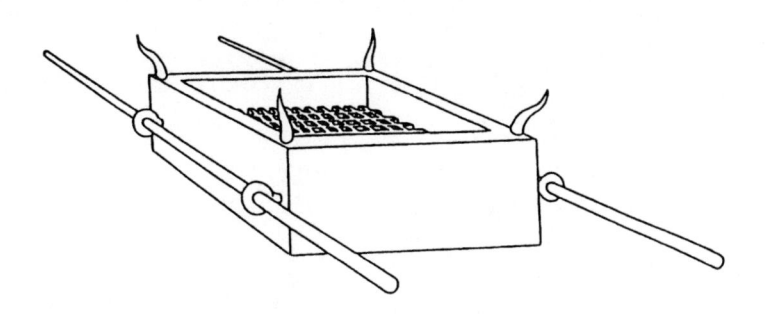

**Jesus,**
**"Appeared to put away sin by the sacrifice of Himself."**
 Heb.9:26


Bible study outline No.2
Brazen Altar in three separate aspects:
**1. Visual illustration.**
   Brazen Altar. Ex.27:1-8; 38:1-7
2. **Type of Christ.**
   Cross upon which Jesus was Crucified.
   Col.1:20; 2:14; Heb.12:2; Jn.19:17,18
3. **Applied to the believer.**
   Jesus died in our place. 1 Cor.15:3,4; Rom.5:6,8
4. **Believer's responsibility.**
   Repent, forsake all your sins and be saved.
   Mk.1:15; Ac.2:38; 3:19; 17:30; 20:21

It was called:
- Altar. Ex.28:43; 29:12
  (for the Lamb) Jn.1:29
- Brazen Altar.Ex.38:30; 39:39
  Brass, the judgment of sin)
- Altar of Shittim Wood. Ex.27:1
  (Christ's Humanity)
- Altar of Burnt-offering.
  Ex.30:28; 3:19; 35:16; 38:1; 40:6
  "Burnt-offering" means "Ascending Offering" showing the acceptance of Christ's Sacrifice by the Father.Isa.53:10; Heb.9:28
- Altar by the Door.Lev.1:5; 4:7
  (Priority of Entrance unto God)

The Brazen Altar was Most Holy. Ex.40:10
It sanctified whatever touched it.
Ex.29:36:37; Mt.23:19
All sacrifices were offered here on this Altar.
Ex.29:38-42; Isa.56:7
Nothing polluted or defective could come near or be offered on it. Lev.22:22; Mal.1:7,8
Nothing blemished or unclean could enter the Presence of God.

---

**The Brazen Altar, is a type of the Cross upon which Jesus was Crucified.** Col.1:20

**"Having made peace through the Blood of His cross."**
  2:14; Heb.12:2

The Hebrew root for altar means "slay" or "slaughter."
The Latin word "alta" means "high."
The Brazen Altar was "the high place of sacrifice (or slaughter)."
Jesus was Lifted up upon the (Altar) Cross at Calvary.

The Altar stood elevated upon the earth, with no steps. Ex.20:26
A type of Golgotha's Hill. (Place of the skull).
Mt.27:33; Mk.15:22; Jn.19:17 "Calvary"

The earth was raised up and whatever was placed upon the Altar was lifted up on high ground.

The Altar lifted the sacrifice as Moses lifted up the serpent in the wilderness. Num.21:4-9 The message for Israel in the wilderness was to look and live.

The message for us is found in Jn.3:14-16
"As Moses lifted up the serpent in the wilderness, even so must the Son of man be lifted up: That whosoever believeth in him should not perish, but have eternal life. For God so loved the world, that he gave his only begotten Son, that whosoever believeth in him should not perish, but have everlasting life.

Jesus said, in Jn.12:32
"If I be lifted up from the earth, will draw all men unto Me." Jesus spoke of His death.

Jn.8:28 He said, "When ye have lifted up the Son of Man, then shall ye know that I Am He,"

Our Altar is the Cross. Our Sacrifice for sin is Jesus Christ. We look to Jesus and live. Jn.3:14-16; 1 Cor.10:9, 10

---

**Lamb, for Sacrifice. A type of Jesus, God's Holy Lamb.**

1. **Visual illustration.**
   Lamb upon the altar for the sacrifice for sin. Ex.29:38-41
2. **Type of Christ.**
   Jesus is the Sacrificed Lamb of God. Jn.1:29,36; Ac.8:32
   The Innocent One who died for us, the guilty.
   1 Pet.1:18,19; 1 Cor.5:7; Heb.9:26; 10:12;
   Eph.5:2; Isa.53:7,11
   Jesus is our sin bearer. Isa.53:4,6,10; Rom.5:6-8;
   2 Cor.5:21; Heb.9:28

3. Applied to the believer.
   Receive God's Sacrifice for sin and receive Salvation.
   2 Cor.6:2; 2 Cor.5:19-21
4. **Believer's responsibility**.
   Reveal Jesus, God's Perfect Lamb for Sacrifice to the world.

A lamb without blemish and without spot was placed upon this Altar for the sacrifice of sin.
Deut.15:21; Lev.22:19-25; Ex.12:1-51; 29:38-41

A type of Christ upon the Cross of Calvary.1 Pet.1:18,19
We are redeemed,
"With the Precious Blood of Christ, as of a lamb without blemish and without spot."Isa.53:7,12

Jn.1:29,
"Behold the lamb of God, which takes away the sin of the world." v.36;1 Cor.5:7; Rev.5:6

The guilty Israelite met God here at the Brazen Altar of Sacrifice to receive forgiveness from sin.

A type pointing to the Cross of Calvary where Jesus became our Supreme Sacrifice for sin.

Located on Golgotha's Hill, nearly 2,000 years ago. Jesus faced that same Fire of God. He met the claims of God for us. The death of an innocent by the shedding of blood for the remission of sins. Jesus the Innocent One died for us, the guilty.

All the unsaved need to do is in faith claim the Sacrifice of Jesus Christ as their Sacrifice. Repent and received forgiveness from their sins.
Isa.53:7; Lk.23:34; Jn.1:29; 2 Cor.5:21; Heb.7:26,27

**Blood**, represents Life

"The life of the flesh is in the blood: and I have given it to you upon the altar to make an atonement for your souls. It is the blood that makes an atonement For the soul." Lev.17:11

**A type of the blood of Christ.**

**Jesus said, "This is My blood of the new testament, which is shed for many for there mission of sins."** Mt.26:28

1. **Visual illustration**.
   The Blood. Lev.17:11
2. **Type of Christ**.
   Jesus shed His Blood Rom.3:24; 1 Pet.1:18,19; Rev.1:5
   Jesus made an Atonement for our soul.
3. **Applied to the believer**.
   Receive His Blood Sacrifice. 1 Jn.1:7,9
   We have been reconciled through the Blood of Christ.
   2 Cor.5:18,19; Col.1:20-23; Heb.9:22,26,28; 10:12
   We are, "Justified by His Blood,"
   "Saved from the wrath of God through Him."Rom.5:9
   We have now received the atonement. v.11
4. **Believer's responsibility**.
   Proclaim the power of His blood to save the world from sin.

The Body of Jesus came from heaven. His Blood was pure, holy, undefiled, and without sin. Mt.1:21; Lk.1:31; Isa.7:14

The Holy Spirit has revealed to us the power of His Blood to wash and cleanse us from our sin. The Life in the Blood of Jesus Christ is a Divine Revelation from God to every born again believer.

Blood is the cleansing agent by which sins are covered or removed. We have been washed in the Blood of the Living Lamb, Jesus Christ. Rev.1:5,6; 5:9 His Blood blots out sin. Ac.3:19; Isa.43:25

Jesus is the only begotten Son of God. The only Person born of a woman whose human nature never came by the ordinary way of generation. His birth was a creation of God. A supernatural act in the womb of the virgin. Jesus was conceived by the power of the

Holy Spirit. He is not of this world. A new thing. A thing that this world had never seen. A happening that has never happened before, nor since. A conception without the aid of man.

The birth of Jesus is the fulfillment of prophecy in the Scriptures.
Isa.7:14; Mt.1:18-23; Jere.31:22

When Jesus came into this world the virgin Mary carried the Perfect Body of Jesus. He already existed before His earthly birth in Bethlehem. He knew before He came down from heaven by the foreknowledge of God that His Father would prepare Him a body not of this world.
Ac.2:23; Mt.26:24; Lk.22:22

In Heb.10:5, "A body hast thou prepared Me."
The pre-existing Life of Christ is recorded in
Mic.5:2; Mt.1:23; Jn.1:1-3,10,14,15; "18:30; 6:62; 7:33; 8:58,14,23,26,27-42; 15:5,8,24; 2 Cor.8:9; Eph.3:9; Phil.2:6-12; Col.1:16-18; 1 Tim.3:16; Heb.1:8; 7:2-4

---

**Physical Characteristics** Ex.27:1-8; 38:1-7
The Altar was 7 ½ feet four-square and 4 ½ feet high. Hollowed with boards. It was made of shittim wood overlaid with brass. The Altar had a horn at each corner on the top of the same wood overlaid with brass. Midst the Altar was a Grate. A network of brass beneath the compass. It was furnished with 4 brazen rings. The rings were attached to the corners of the grate through openings on two sides. Two staves were inserted on each side with which to bear the Altar. The staves were made of the same materials as the Altar. All the utensils: the pans, shovels, basins, fleshhooks, and the fire pans were made of brass.

**Size**
The Brazen Altar was four-square.
**Four**, speaks of Weakness and Yieldingness.
Jesus became weak and yielded everything to God, because He wanted to:

In Jn.10:17,18 Jesus said,
"My Father loves Me, because I lay down My life, that I might take it again. No man takes it from Me, but I lay it down of Myself. I have power to lay it down, and I have power to take it again. This commandment have I received of My Father."
Mt.27:14; 26:53; 2 Cor.13:4; Isa.53:7

The Grace of God is found in His Only Begotten Son, Jesus Christ. Jn.1:14,17
"The law was given by Moses, but grace and truth came by
  Jesus Christ. 1 Tim.2:5

The Brazen Altar was large enough to hold all the other pieces of Furniture of the Tabernacle, speaks of all our blessings flow through His Precious Blood Atonement upon the Cross of Calvary. The entire Gospel message of Jesus Christ is found in types here in the Brazen Altar of burnt offering.

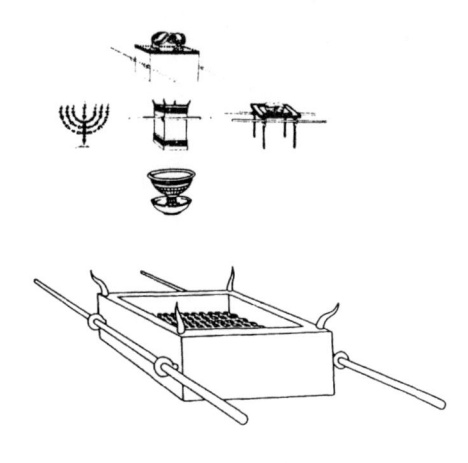

**Material**
The Altar was made of a white incorruptible wood. It has a very hard, durable substance. It can withstand heat and stand up to a great amount of punishment. Jesus. took a tremendous beating to redeem us.

**Wood**, speaks of Humanity.
The Perfect incorruptible, sinless humanity of Jesus. The Body of Jesus was sinless.

Jesus is without sin.
2 Cor.5:21; Heb.1:9; 7:26-28; 4:15; 9:14; 1 Jn.3:5

Jesus is, "Of the Holy Spirit." Mt.1:20; Lk.1:35

The wood came from the acacia tree which grew in the desert. This desert shrub has a long tap root that reaches way down into the subterranean dampness.
It speaks of Jesus as "A root out of dry ground:" Isa.53:2

**Brass, speaks of His Suffering.**
Ac.3:18
"But those things, which God before had showed by the mouth of all His prophets, that Christ should suffer, He hath so fulfilled." Heb.2:18; 5:8

Examples:
- They spit on Him. Lk.18:32
- They tried to push Him off a hill top in Nazareth. Lk.4:29
- A cloth was put over His head and they punched Him in the face and said, "If you be the Son of God, tell us who hit you." Mt.26:67,68

- His beard was plucked from His face. Isa.50:6 (prophecy).
- Jesus prayed at the Mount of Olives
    "Being in an agony Jesus prayed more earnestly: and His sweat was as it were great drops of blood falling to the ground." Lk.22:44
- He was betrayed with a kiss. Mt.26:48
- He had three trials in one night.
- They planted a crown of thorns upon His head, and a reed in His right hand: they bowed their knees before Him and mocked Him, saying, Hail, King of the Jews. Mt.27:29
- They tried Him to the whipping post and with 39 lashes they ripped open His flesh and His precious Innocent Blood streamed down His sacrificial body.
    Mt.27:26; Mk.15:15
- Nails were driven into His hands and feet. Jn.20:25-27
- All His joints were pulled out of place.
  Ps.22:14 (Not a bone in His body was broken)
- A soldier with his spear pierced His side and His blood and water flowed. Jn.19:34
- His visage was married more than that of any man. Isa.52:14 in prophecy Etc.

Jesus conquered every sickness and disease for us on the Cross of Calvary.

Isa.53:5
  "Jesus was wounded for our transgressions. He was bruised for our iniquities: the chastisement of our peace was upon Him; and with His stripes we ar healed."

1 Pet.2:24
  "Who His Own Self (Jesus) bare our sins in His Own Body on the tree, that we, being dead to sins, should live unto righteousness by whose stripes ye were healed."

The lamb upon the altar went to be sacrificed willingly. Jesus went to be sacrificed for the sins of the whole world, willingly. He suffered greatly to redeem us. As the redeemed we must be willing to serve Him.

The Brazen Altar was Hollow,
speaks of Christ Emptied Himself. Phil.2:6,7
We are crucified with Christ. Gal.2:20; Rom.6:11,2

**Location**
The Brazen Altar was located at the east end of the Outer Court. It was placed directly in front of the Gate of Entrance on the inside of the Outer Court. This is what the guilty Israelite faced upon entering in through the Gate.
When the Holy Spirit convicts a person of their sins they face the blood sacrifice of Jesus at the altar of Calvary.

**Purpose**
The purpose of the Altar was to receive the sacrifices on it. To slay and sprinkle the blood and to make an atonement for sin. It was the place of death and blood shedding for the sins of the people. The innocent had to face the knife of the priest and the fire of God's judgment for the guilty.

The guilty Israelite brought an innocent sacrifice to this Altar. He then laid his hand upon the head of the sacrifice and claimed it as his substitute for sin. The sacrifice was then slain, the blood was shed and the penalty for sin was made. Lev.1:3,4; 3:2,8,13

A type pointing to the Cross of Calvary where Jesus became our Supreme Sacrifice. Our Substitute for sin.

Horns, are a symbol of Power.
Ps.18:2
Christ is the "Horn (Power) of Salvation." Lk.1:68,69

There were four horns on the Altar. They were made of one piece with the Altar. The horns were made of shittim wood, overlaid with brass. Four horns on the four corners. Here at the Brazen Altar the horns, speak of the power God used in raising Jesus from the dead. Mt.28:6; 12:40; 16:21; Lk.24:6

The same power God used in raising Christ from the dead is the same power that He will use in raising us up at the "Last Day." The same Spirit that dwells in Jesus, dwells in us.

The horns on the Altar pointed upward and outward. They were sprinkled with the blood of the sacrifice. Ex.29:12 They pointed to the four corners of the earth.

A type of Christ and His message. The power in the blood of Jesus saves from sin.

Jesus tells us what to do. 1 Tim.2:4; 2 Pet.3:9; Jn.20:21

"Go ye therefore, and teach all nations,"Mt.28:19; Lk.9:60

It is God's will to: "Have all men to be saved, and to come unto the knowledge of the truth." 1 Tim.2:4

"Not willing that any should perish, but that all should come to repentance." 2 Pet.3:9

14:23
"Go out into the highways and hedges, and compel them to come in, that my house may be filled."

Jn.20:21
"Peace be unto you: as My Father hath sent Me, even so send I you."

**Ropes,** bound the sacrifice to the horns of the Altar. Ps.118:27
The sacrifice was bound to the horns with strong cords until it's life was taken.

A type of Christ. The nails driven into His hands and feet did not hold Him to the Cross of Calvary.

It was love that bound our Savior to the Cross until His Life was taken. Freely given up for us by the shedding of His Own Blood.

Rom.5:8
"God commended his love toward us, in that, while we were yet sinners, Christ died for us."

1 Jn.4:9
"In this was manifested the love of God toward us, because that God sent his only begotten Son into the world, that we might live through him."

1 Jn.4:8
"He that loves not knows not God: for God is love."

"We love Him, because He first loved us." 1 Jn.4:19 -21.

When we received Christ we received God's love.

**Rings**
There were four rings of brass. Two rings on each side in the four corners. They were one complete piece with the Grate.

Rings, upon the net, speak of Jesus
"Obtained Eternal Redemption." For us through His Blood.
Heb.9:12

**Staves**
The two Staves, speak of His Death and Resurrection.

In the New Testament whenever His death is mentioned the fact of His Resurrection always follows.

Example:
1 Cor.15:3, 4
"I delivered unto you first of all that which I also received, how that Christ died for our sins according to the scriptures; And that He was buried, and that He rose again the third day according to he scriptures:"

If Christ be not risen, our faith is in vain. 1 Cor.15:14,17

**The Rings and Staves together**,
speak of the Gospel of the kingdom carried, without end to this world. Mk.16:15

The **Fire** on the Brazen Altar is the symbol of the Presence of God, Holy and Eternal. Heb.12:29

God lit His Fire on the Brazen Altar, directly from heaven or from within the Holy of Holies upon the Mercy Seat with His Shekinah Glory between the two Cherubim upon the Ark.

Lev.9:23, 24
"There came a fire out from before the Lord, and consumed upon the Altar the burnt-offering and the fat: which when all the people saw, they shouted, and fell on their faces."
It was God's Fire. Redemption is is God's plan.

God lit His Fire, because He is the Author of salvation. We see this in the typology of the Brazen Altar where the Godhead is glorified in redemption.

We see in the Godhead
1. God, the Father planned His great plan of redemption.
2. God, the Son Jesus Christ fulfilled His Father's plan of redemption.
3. God, the Holy Spirit witnesses to this redeeming fact in the Scriptures.
   The Father gave us the Sacrifice.
   Jesus is the Sacrifice.
   The Holy Spirit reveals the Sacrifice.
   Col.2:9; Rom.1:20; Ac.17:29; 1 Jn.5:7,8

Lev.6:13
"The fire shall ever be burning upon the altar; it shall never go out."
Even on the march the Fire was kept alive with live coals.
They were carried from place to place.

A continual fire demanded a continual sacrifice for sin,
speaks of God's continual call to repent. To the Israelites in the Old Testament it was a reminder to bring a sacrifice for sin. To the unsaved and non-believer today in the New Testament it is a reminder in type to repent and forsake their sins, receive Christ and be saved.
God's Fire is kept alive today burning in Christ.
Mt.3:11; Ac.4:31; 8:15-17; 9:17; 10:44; 19:2

**A Live Coal**, was carried from place to place in a fire pan to keep the fire burning continually.
The Holy Spirit is God's Fire. Christ is in us, and we are filled with the power of the Holy Spirit to carry the continual call to this present evil world to repent and receive Christ.

Lev.9:23,24 Jeremiah said, "His Word was in my heart as a burning Fire shut up in my bones," 20:9
This Fire is the Holy Spirit.

John the Baptist said, "I indeed baptize you with water unto repentance, but Jesus that comes after me is mightier then I, whose shoes I am not worthy to bear: He shall baptize you with the Holy Spirit, and with Fire." Mt.3:11; Mk.1:8

This was fulfilled on the Day of Pentecost.
Ac.2:2,3; 4:31; 10:44-48; 19:6

When we received Christ, we received the power of the Holy Spirit.
Rom.8:9-16; 1 Jn.4:13; 3:24; Ps.104:4; Heb.1:7
The witness of Jesus is in us. Rev.19:10

The Continual Fire
1. It was the responsibility of the priest to keep the fire burning. Lev.6:12,13
   It is up to us to keep the Fire of the Holy Spirit burning, and the Gospel message of Jesus Christ alive within us.
2. The Fire is God's Holy Nature. He burns out sin. The power of His Spirit does this in us. We are His holy vessels).
3. His Fire spreads to the Golden Altar, and to the Candlestick. His Fire is alive in our prayer life, and in our life and light to the world, which is Christ within us.
4. His Fire: Purifies. Num.31:21-23
   Reveals. Ex.3:3; 19:18; Isa.6:4; Ezek.1:4
   Transfigures. Mal.3:2,3; 2 Cor.3:18
5. God lit His Fire. Lev.9:24   He lights us up. It is our responsibility to seek God to keep His Fire burning within us. Rom.12:1; Eph.5:1;Lev.1:9
6. There are many places in the Bible where the Fire fell. Lev.9:22-24; 2 Chron.7:1-3; 1 Kgs.18:38,39; 1 Chron.21:26
   God's Fire fell on the Day of Pentecost, and has been falling ever since.

**Consumed**
The sacrifices were consumed by fire upon the Altar. Lev.1:8,9

The term "burnt offering" means, "ascending offering" showing the acceptance of Christ's Sacrifice by the Father.
Isa.53:10; Heb.9:28

It was a sweet smelling savor, speaks of Jesus in
Eph.5:2
"Walk in love, as Christ also hath loved us, and hath given Himself for us an offering and a sacrifice to God for a sweet smelling savour."

This applies to the believer. 2 Cor.2:14-16
"We are unto God a sweet savor of Christ,"
  1 Cor.15:10; 1 Pet.2:7,8

**Grate**
Midst the Altar was a Grate. The Altar was 4 ½ ft. high. The Grate was placed 2 ft. 3 ins. from the top and 2 ft. 3 ins. from the bottom. This placed the Grate directly in the middle of the Altar. Half-way up, inside the Altar was the Grate to hold the sacrifice.

The Mercy Seat in the Holy of Holies is a type of God's throne on earth, was placed upon the Ark. The Ark was 2 ft. 3 ins. high. The Grate was on the same level as the Mercy Seat. The sacrifice was placed upon the Grate.

The supreme Sacrifice of Jesus Christ upon the Cross of Calvary was equal to the throne of God. Jesus met the claims of His Father. Death by the shedding of Blood by His Innocent Lamb to Atone for sin.

**Ashes**
The ashes were carried out before the entire nation of Israel and buried in a clean dry place. It was a solemn funeral, speaks, of the Body of Jesus. After the Sacrifice of Jesus, His Body was taken down off the Cross and laid in a clean, dry place (new tomb). Mt.27:58-66; Mk.6:29

The Brazen Altar, was covered with:
1. A purple cloth.
2. A badger's skin. when carried from place to place while on the march (journey).

All prophecy that applies to redemption in Christ has already been fulfilled with only one exception. The redemption of our bodies. 1 Cor.15:51; 1 Thess.4:16,17; Lk.17:24; Mt.24:27

# Chapter 3

**The Laver, speaks of Cleansing and Sanctification.**

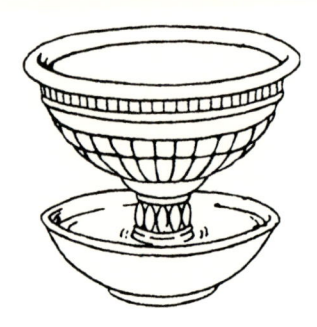

**Jesus is our cleansing and daily sanctification.**
Jn.15:3; 17:17

Bible study outline No.3
1. **Visual illustration**.
   Laver, (of brass). Ex.30:17-21; 38:8
2. **Type of Christ**.
   Jesus is our Cleansing. 1 Jn.1:9; Ps.51:2; Heb.13:12
3. **Applied to the believer**.
   We are cleansed and washed through the Word of God.
   Jn.15:3; Eph.5:25-27; Heb.10:22; Ps.51:10
   Sanctification.1 Cor.6:11; 1:30,2
4. **Believer's responsibility**.
   Live a separated and holy life before God and before the world. 2 Cor.6:17; 1 Thess.4:3-7; Rev.18:4,5

Aaron and his sons were brought to the Curtain Door of the Tabernacle and were washed with water from the laver. Ex.29:4 The Laver is a type of God's Holy Word. We are cleansed with a washing of water by His Word. Eph.5:25,26

**The priest washed:**
- before consecration. Ex.40:12
- before entering the Tabernacle. Ex.30:19,20
- before approaching the Brazen Altar. Ex.30:20

This was done in order for the priest to be able to serve people in their daily sacrifices.
A type of God's people receiving a washing of water by His Word to minister.

**Physical Characteristics** Ex.30:17-21; 38:8
Laver, Heb. Something round, a basin. The Laver was round and hollow, with the water able to run on to the hands and feet. The "foot" support was circular in shape and formed another basin at the bottom. It was an expansion of the shaft with a turned up rim. The Laver and his foot were made of brass. A double bowl. It consisted of two parts together. The Laver Proper and his Stand.

**Size**
The Lord gave no specific measurements for the laver, because God's provision for cleansing is unlimited. The Word of God and the Holy Spirit cannot be measured. The divine cannot be measured by the human. True holiness is not a man made set of specifications. True holiness flows from the nature of Christ within and without and is a separated walk. 1 Cor.1:30; Mt.5:17 20; Isa.45:18; 54:17; 64:6; Mt.23:25-28; Lk.18:9-14
The laver is for the priestly believer.
Ex.19:1-6; 1 Pet.2:5-9; Rev.1:6

It was the only piece of furniture of the Tabernacle that was not covered either on the march or when it was set up for service. The laver was always open to view. There is a constant open revelation of the anointed Word to the world through us in the fullness of His Spirit. The revelation of God's Word purifies. Isa.6:1-7

We are an open face people to bring God's glory to this present evil world with a clean mind. A pure heart and spirit.
Mt.5:8
"Lets cleanse ourselves from all filthiness of the flesh and spirit, perfecting holiness in the fear of God."
2 Cor.7:1; Heb.12:1

Jesus Christ is God's cleansing for us. We have been washed in His Precious Blood. We stay clean at the Laver through Christ with His daily washing of water by the Word. This world and the evils thereof do not affect our standing before God. Heb.10:14 We belong to God and are set apart from this present evil world. The words and actions of people do not interfere with our communion with God. The present evils will only if we let them. There is no limit to the purity of our heart. This is why the Laver was not covered.

We are opened faced before God and before the world. We excel in God, through Christ, by the power of the Holy Spirit. We are separated from the world and separated unto God. We are what God has called us to be. Clean vessels
Isa.52:11; Jn.15:3; 13:10

**Materials**
The Laver and his foot were made of brass from the mirrors of the women. Highly polished copper mirrors called looking glasses. Ex.38:8

These women made a great sacrifice. They gave up their mirrors to make God's Laver.

We look at ourselves in God's mirror to see if we reflect the image of Jesus Christ. We give way to the power of the Holy Spirit to mold us and shape us into the image of Christ by the washing of water by His Word. Those who love the meeting place of God sacrifice a means of vanity to produce a vessel of cleansing. The mirror is the Word of God. Jas.1:23-25

Our approach to God is in holiness. The mirror reveals our need for daily cleansing and the water provides the means for cleansing. The water is the Word of God and the Holy Spirit. Eph.5:26,27; Jn.7:37-39

The Word and the Spirit are in agreement. They work together for the purpose of our cleansing.

The water for the Laver was obtained from the smitten rock, that Rock is Christ. 1 Cor.10:4; Ex.17:6; Ps.78:20; Jn.19:34

"This is He that came by water and blood, even Jesus Christ; not by water only but by water and blood. And it is the spirit that bears witness, because the spirit is truth. For there are three that bear record in heaven, the Father, the word, and the Holy Spirit: and these three are one. And there are three that bear witness in earth, the spirit, and the water, and the blood: and these three agree in one." 1 Jn.5:6-8

The laver without it's foot would fall.
Christ is the ground,
support and foundation of our sanctification as well as our justification. Jude 24; 1 Cor.1:30; Rom.16:25

**Location**
The Laver was located on the ground in the Outer Court between the Brazen Altar and the Tabernacle Proper. Ex.30:18; 40:7,30
It was located there for convenience. A constant reminder for the need of cleansing. Always available for the priests to wash when they go from the Brazen Altar to the Tabernacle, so that they die not. Ex.30:20,21; 40:32

Our Bibles should be in reach for a constant reminder for daily cleansing. Our Laver is the Word of God and should be within our reach. At our convenience.
Ps.119:9; Jn.15:3;Eph.5:26
The laver also speaks of **Practical Salvation**.

**Purpose**
The purpose of the Laver was for the priests to wash their hands and feet daily for ministering at the Brazen Altar and in the Holy Place. Ex.40:12; 30:19; Ps.26:6; 119:9

The laver was filled with water for cleansing. The top and bottom. The base of the Laver was for the priest to wash themselves. The top was kept pure and refilled as necessary.

Water in the upper part of the Laver,
speaks of Christ in heaven, the true, pure water of life.

Water in the lower part of the Laver,
speaks of Christ on earth in His humiliation. Jn.7:37-39
Water in the Laver is, a plain figure of the written Word.

The Laver teaches of our need for daily, cleansing. This is not cleansing from the guilt of sin, but from the defilements of the way. We come in contact with those that are dead in trespasses and sins.
1 Jn.5:19
"The whole world lieth in wickedness."

The priest did not wash in the Laver, but from it. They drew water from the top to wash and were cleansed from the bottom. Only from the foot of the Laver did they wash.

Eph.5:26 that Jesus,
"Might sanctify and cleanse us with the washing of water by His Word," Jn.13:5-11

Those who serve in God's House should not go to Church to get a cleansing or refreshment, but bring it with them. The Word of God washes, cleanses and sanctifies us as we obey His truth.
1 Pet.1:22

We have constant communion with God by living in the spirit of the Laver, that is in His Word.

1 Jn.1:9
"If we confess our sins, He is faithful and just to forgive us our sins, and to cleanse us from all unrighteousness."

We read God's Word to see how clean we really are. We compare ourselves to Jesus. He is our example of what we are to be. Our one desire is to be like Jesus.

The Lord tells us to look into His Word that we may know Him. Phil.3:9,10

The priest were forgiven of their sins through a blood sacrifice at the Brazen Altar. They washed at the Laver and were clean to serve in the Holy Place.

A type of the believer. We have received forgiveness from our sins at the Cross of Calvary through the Blood of Christ.
We receive a daily washing of water by His Word to serve in His Church.

A Bible Study Outline
The Laver is a type of:
(1) A Cleansing by His Word.
   Ps.119:9; Jn.15:3;17:17,19; Eph.5:26

(2) His Word is a Mirror.
   Jas.1:23-25
   In which we see ourselves.
   1 Cor.13:12

(3) God's two-fold provision for Cleansing:
   a. At the Brazen Altar, (A type of the Cross) through the Cleansing of the Blood of Christ.
   Eph.1:20
   b. At the Laver
      (A type of the Word of God)
      by a washing of water by His Word
      Eph.5:26
      Blood and Water.
      Lev.14:5-7; Heb.9:19; Jn.19:34;
      1 Jn.5:6-8; Rev.7:14

# Chapter 4

**The Curtain Door** _____

**Holy Place, speaks of His Church (the Body of Christ).**

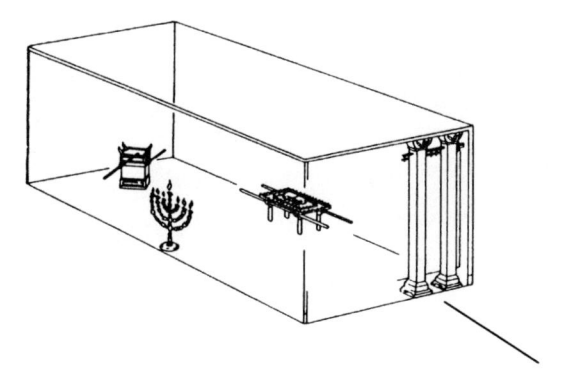

Curtain Door

Holy Place. Ex.26:35; Heb.9:2
It contained three pieces of furniture:
1. Candlestick.
2. Table of Shewbread.
3. Golden Altar.
   Ex.26:35; 40:22,24,26; Heb.9:2 KJV


It was called:
Inner Court.
Sanctuary. Heb.9:2
First Tabernacle. Heb.9:6

The Holy Place was located at the east end. It was 30 ft. long and 15 ft. high and wide.

## JESUS PRAYED FOR HIS CHURCH.
   (Jn.17:20-26

He ask that the Father unify the Church.
   (17:20-22)

He asks that the Church honor the Son.
   (17:21)

He asks that the Church display God's Love.
   (17:23)

He asks that the Church experience God's Love.
   (17:25, 26)

He asks that the Church enjoy Christ's Glory in
   Heaven forever. (17:24)

We are His Church of born again believers. We are called to worship and serve.

"Not forsaking the assembling of ourselves together, as the
   manner of some is; but exhorting one another: and s much
   the more, as ye see the day approaching." Heb 10:25

**Curtain Door, was the entrance into the Holy Place.**

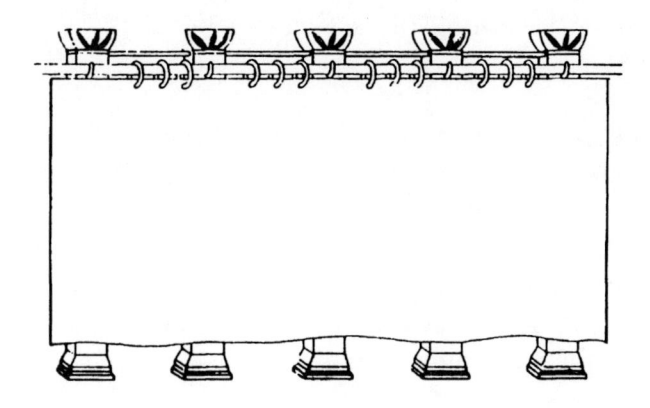

**Jesus is the Door of Service through the Holy Spirit.**
Jn.10:9

Bible study outline No.4
1. **Visual illustration**.
   Curtain Door. Ex.26:36,37; 36:37,38
2. **Type of Christ.**
   Jesus is the Door of Service through the Holy Spirit.
   Jn.10:9; 14:14-26
3. **Applied to the believer**.
   Enter in to Serve and Worship. Ac.20:34,35
4. **Believer's responsibility**.
   Answer the Call to Worship.
   1 Pet.2:9; 2 Pet.1:3,4; Gal.5:13; Heb.9:14; 12:28; Col.3:24

It was called:
1. Hangings for the Door of the Tent. Ex.26:36
2. Hanging. Ex.26:37
3. Hanging for the Tabernacle Door. Ex.36:37
4. Door of the Tabernacle of the Congregation. Lev.1:3

**Physical Characteristics.** Ex.26:36,37; 36:37,38
The Curtain Door was 15 ft. wide and 15 ft. high. It was made of fine twined linen of white, blue, purple and scarlet of needlework.
The Curtain Door hangings of the Holy Place was white, blue, purple and scarlet, suspended by gold rings with gold fillets from five pillars of shittim wood overlaid with gold with five sockets of brass at their bases.

**The colors of the Curtain Door were**:
**White**, speaks of His Purity.
Heb.4:15 Jesus, "Was in all points tempted like as we are, yet without sin." 1 Jn.3:5; 1 Pet.2:22.; 2 Cor.5:21
   We have His Purity in us.
**Blue**, speaks of Jesus, the Heavenly One.

   The Only Begotten Son of God, the Christ.
   Jn.6:33,38; 3:13
   Through Jesus, we are a heavenly people.
**Purple**, speaks of Jesus the King of kings.
   Lk.23:38; Mk.15:26; Mt.27:37; Jn.19:14,19

**Scarlet**, speaks of Jesus the Son of Man. Servant obedient unto death. Suffering in the past."
1 Cor.5:7; Heb.10:12
Jesus said, "The servant is not above his Lord."
Mt 10:24 We rejoice that we are accounted worthy to be persecuted for His Name sake.

**Size**
The Curtain Door was smaller in width than the Outer Court Gate. Only the priest were allowed to enter into the Holy Place to serve.

Only those who have been washed in the Blood of the Lamb, Jesus Christ and
"Study to shew thyself approved unto God, a workman that needs not to be ashamed, rightly dividing the word of truth" are permitted to minister and serve in the Church that Jesus died for. 2 Tim.2:15

**Material**
The Curtain Door was made of fine twined linen of needlework, **speaks of Righteousness.**

**Located**
The Curtain Door hung on the east end of the Tabernacle Proper.

**Purpose**
The Curtain Door was the entrance to the Holy Place and received all the priests who entered in to serve.

Everyone who has been saved by the blood of God's holy Lamb, Jesus Christ is a minister of God Word.

We,
"Both (Jews and Gentle) have access by One Spirit unto the father." Eph. 2:18

We enter in to serve, through Christ, in the power, influence, direction and living by the Holy Spirit.

**Curtain Door Pillar,
the Lord Jesus Christ is our strong Pillar.**

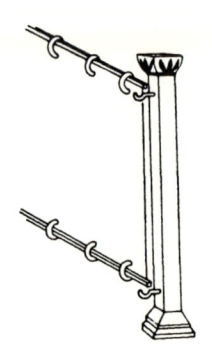

**Believers are called pillars.** Gal.2:9
Examples
The Five Pillars upon which the Curtain Door hung were made of shittim wood overlaid with gold.

These Five Pillars, speak of the five prophetic Names of Jesus in Isa.9:6
1. Wonderful. 2. Counselor. 3. The Mighty God.
4. Everlasting Father. 5. The Prince of Peace.

They also speak of Jesus our:
1. Saviour. Lk.2:10-12; 19:10
2. Sanctifier. Jn.17:17-19; 1 Cor.1:30
3. Healer. Isa.53:5; 1 Pet.2:24
4. Baptizer in the Holy Spirit.
   Jn.1:32,33; Ac.1:5,8; 2:16-19,38,39
5. Soon Coming King.
   1 Cor.15:51-57; 1 Thes.4:13-18

We are: 1. Saved. 2. Sanctified. 3. Healed.
4. Filled with the Spirit. 5. Waiting for our Soon Coming King.

Rev.22:20
   Jesus, "Testifies these things saith, surely I come quickly. Amen, Even so, come lord Jesus."

1. **Pillars**, represent His Church.
   God's Church is the pillar and ground of truth in this world.
   1 Tim.3:15; Rev.3:12

These Five Pillars, speak of the five evangelists of the epistles in the New Testament who held up Christ as their example. Peter, James, John, Paul and Jude. Three of these writers are called pillars in His Church. Gal.2:9

We are His pillars that reflect and represent our Great Pillar Jesus Christ.

2. Their Five Sockets (solid brass). Ex.26:37; 36:38
   Brass, speaks of Suffering. Rev.1:15; 2:18; Dan.10:6
   a. speaks of the judgment of God according to righteousness upon Jesus. He suffered for us by taking upon Himself our judgment for sin so that we may be partakers of His Righteousness. 2 Cor.5:21
   b. We may be partakers of the righteousness of God through Him. 2 Cor.5:19-21

   We will face judgment for sin. Judgment begins at the House of God. 1 Pet.4:17
   We are to judge ourselves in the light of God's Word. 1 Cor.6:1-5
   If we judge ourselves we will not be judged.
   1 Cor.11:31

The five pillars rested upon the five sockets of brass, speak of His Endurance.
a. Jesus suffered to redeem us. Jn.5:16
b. As the redeemed we must be willing to serve Him.
   2 Tim.3:12
   "All that will live godly in Christ Jesus shall suffer persecution."

   Mt.5:10, 11
   "We are blessed when we suffer for His Holy Name's sake."

3. Their Hooks (gold, upon which the Curtain Door hung). Ex.26:37; 36:38
   Speak of the very Heart and Design of God.
a. Jesus is the very Heart and Design of God in His Church. His Father said in Mt.3:17
   "This is my beloved Son, in whom I am well pleased."
 b. Jesus is our only example of how we are to live and serve in His Church.

4. Their Five **Chapters**. Ex.36:38
   Wood, overlaid with gold.
   a. Speak of His Crowing Evidence.
      Jesus Crowned with Glory and Honor. Rev.5:13
   b. After we have received our crown (rewards) we will place them at the Feet of Jesus. Rev.4:10,11

**Five Crowns for believers.**
1. Crown of Life,
    "Endure Temptation."
        Jas.1:12; Rev.2:10
2. Crown of Glory,
    "Elder's Pastor's crown."
        1 Pet.5:2-4
3. Crown of Rejoicing,
    "Soul Winner's crown."
        1 Thes.2:19,20; Phil.4:1
4. Crown of Righteousness,
    "Love His Appearing."
        2 Thes.4:8
5. Crown Incorruptible,
    "Victor's Crown."
        1 Cor.9:25-27
   We will cast our crowns before the Throne,
      at the feet of Jesus.
        Rev.4:10

5. Their **Fillets**, wood overlaid with gold   (connected the
   pillars) of the Curtain Door,Ex.36:38
   Fillets, also speak of Fellowship.
a. Jesus has a Perfect Fellowship with His Father. He did
   also when He was on this earth in the Flesh.
   Jn.10:30 (Godhead. Col.2:9; Rom.1:20)
   Jesus fellowshipped, labored and served to bring all the
   glory and Honor to His Father.
b. We fellowship in Jesus. We have a perfect
   fellowship with God in Christ by the power of the Holy
   Spirit (the Godhead) and with all God's people.
   1 Jn.3,7; Ac.2:42  To bring Him Glory!

We have the fellowship:
- of His Son Jesus Christ our Lord. 1 Cor.1:9
- of the ministering to the saints. 2 Cor.8:4
- of the mystery, ... whole family. Eph.3:9,15
- in the Gospel. Phil.1:5; 4:3
- of the Spirit. Phil.2:1
- of His sufferings. Phil.3:10

We fellowship in His Church. Heb.10:25; 1 Cor.10:17
- together in Christ Phile.23,24; 1 Cor.3:9

**The Table of Shewbread, was food for the priests.**

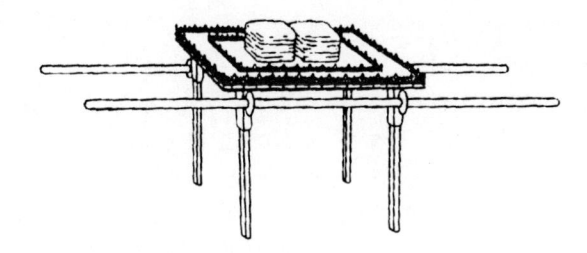

**Jesus said, "I AM the Bread of Life." Jn.6:35**

Bible study outline No.5
1. **Visual illustration**.
   The Table of Shewbread.Ex.25:23-29; 37:10-16
2. **Type of Christ**.
   Jesus is the Bread of Life. Jn.6:35,48
3. **Applied to the believer**.
   Eat the Bread of Life which came down from heaven and never hunger. Jn.6:32-58
4. **Believer's responsibility**.
   Give this Bread to all who hunger and thirst after righteousness. Jn.21:15-17; Eph.4:16; Mt.5:6

It was called:
 - Table of Shewbread. Ex.25:30
   (Emphasizing bread)
 - Table of Shittim. Wood. Ex.25:23; 37:10
   (Word made Flesh)
 - Pure Table. Lev.24:6
   (Holy, must be clean to partake)

- Table. Ex.39:36; 40:4,22
  (One Bread, One Body)
- Table of Gold. 1 Kgs.7:48
  (Emphasizing His Divine Nature)

**Physical Characteristics** Ex.25:23-30; 37:10-16
The Table of Shewbread was made of shittim wood, overlaid with pure gold and had a double crown. A crown of gold around it. It had a border of an hand breadth round about and a golden crown to the border thereof round about it. It had two staves of shittim wood overlaid with gold and four rings of gold in the four corners (on the feet) in which the staves were inserted. The Table was 3 ft. long. 1½ ft. wide and 2 ft. 3 ins. high. The vessels for the Table were: dishes (chargers) for holding, and conveying the bread. Num.7:13,18,19 Spoons for the frankincense (incense). Lev.24:7 Num.7:14,20,26; Lev.24:7 Covers and bowls, (cups) for the wine. Num.6:15; 28:7,14; Lev.23:18

**Size**
The Table was small with a limited area, but large enough for all who have been redeemed with the precious Blood of our Lord and Savior, Jesus Christ. It was small enough to exclude all those who reject His Blood Sacrifice for sin. The Table with it's small size shows that few experience real fellowship with God.

The Lord's Supper was instituted by Jesus. Mt.26:17-30; Mk.14:12-26; Lk.22:7-30; Jn.13:1-30
It is recorded in 1 Cor.11:23-32

We observe the Table of the Lord often for Christ is revealed at the Table. Lk.24:35; 2 Pet.2:13; Jn.12

It was a Table of communion and fellowship. Here we have fellowship with the Lord and with one another. 1 Jn.1:1-4
The closeness around the Table, speaks of our communion with Christ and His Church. 1 Cor.10:20-22; 11:23-30
We gather as priests unto Jesus.
1 Pet.2:9; Ps.89:7; Jn.6:35,41,48,50,51
Our fellowship is centered in His Person. Only Christ the Bread of Life can satisfy, nourish and deliver us.

All things are on His Table of provision.
S.S.1:12; 1 Kgs.2:22-27; Mt.6:11; Phil.4:4:19

1 Cor.11:28,29
"Let a man examine himself, and so let him eat of that bread, and drink of that cup. For he that eats and drinks unworthy, eats and drinks damnation to himself, not discerning the Lord's body."

To partake in understanding and being worthy can result in healing and life. To partake of the Table in ignorance and unworthiness can result in sickness and death.
Lev.21:21; 1 Cor.11:30

**Material**
The Table was made of Shittim Wood overlaid with gold:
**Gold**, speaks of His Divine Nature.
**Wood**, speaks of His Human Nature.

The material for the Shewbread was provided by the people.
Lev.24:8; Neh.10:32,33

Twelve cakes of fine flour was prepared by the Levites.
Lev.24:5-9; 1 Chron.9:32; 23:29
It was placed in two rows of six loaves on the Table.
Ex.25:30; 40:23; Lev.24:6

Zech.12:10; Lk.2:35
Pure, incorruptible bread, speaks of God's Covenant.

**Leaven** was excluded. Lev.2:11
speaks of Corruption (tradition) 1 Cor.5:7,8

**The Meal Offering**, also speaks of the "First-fruits."

As a meal offering. A type of His Resurrection.
"Part, ... in pieces" the loaf or cake, is a type of Broken Bread.

The Threefold Meal Offering, speaks of His Sufferings:
"Pan" (flat plate)
speaks of Christ's Sufferings in His body.

"Fryingpan" (pan) speaks of Christ's Sufferings in His Soul.

"Baked" speaks of Christ's Suffering in His Spirit.

**Twelve**, speaks of Divine Order and Governmental Perfection.

Jesus fed His Bread (Word) through His twelve apostles.
Mt.14:15-21
We eat the Word of Christ by the power of the Holy Spirit in this day.

The twelve tribes of Israel were represented by the twelve loaves. One loaf for each tribe.

**One crumb brought healing and deliverance
We have the whole loaf in Christ**. Mk.7:24-30

The Bread of God which is Jesus is before us at all times. We eat His Word He has given through the power of the Holy Spirit.

**Location**
The Table was located on the north side of the Holy Place.
Ex.40:22; Heb.9:2

**"Shewbread before Me Always"** Ex.25:30
Jesus was always before His Father. We are always before the Lord. Jn.1:18
The Church exhibits the life, death, resurrection and coming again of Jesus. 1 Cor.11:26; Rom.6:4

**Shewbread** literally means, "Bread of the Faces"
2 Cor.4:6; Rev.22:4
Jesus was always before His Father's Face.
We are always before our Lord's Face.

**"Bread of the Presence."** (Heb.) Lev.24:8
Jesus is always in the Father's Presence.
The Lord meets with us at the Table of communion:
We are always in the presence of the Lord through Christ.

**"Holy Bread"** 1 Sam.21:4-6
  Jesus is the holy one of God. Mk.1:24; Lk.4:34
We are holy in Him.

**"Bread of Order"**.
There is order at the Table of the Lord.
2 Chron.13:11; 1 Cor.11:34

There is order in the Body of Christ. Eph.4:11
"God is not the author of confusion, but of peace, as in all churches of the saints." 1 Cor.14:33

**"Bread of God"** Lev.21:21
Jesus is our Living Bread. In Jn.6:51 He said,
"I Am the living bread which came down from heaven: if any man eat of this bread, he shall live for ever: and the bread that I will give is My flesh, which I will give for the life of the world."

**"Perpetual Bread**. Num.4:7
Jesus said, for us to eat of the Heavenly Bread and never hunger. Jn.6:51-57

He is our daily Bread. Mt.6:11

The Bread of His Body is constantly renewed. Jn.6:35

**Continued Bread** Num.4:7
The priests substituted new loaves for old each Sabbath with the change of priests.

The New Testament (Covenant) brought a new bread, which is Christ and a new priesthood.
Christ is the Everlasting Bread.

To partake of Christ is to be actively and submissively involved in His Church.

We are by nature what we eat. We eat the Bread of Life and partake together.
Eating something that is impure defiles our bodies and makes us sick even unto death.
Impure acts, words and thoughts defiles our spirit.
1 Cor.11:28,29

We do godly acts, contain holy and kind words, good thoughts and fellowship together for His Glory.

Jesus said, "**I AM the bread of Life.**" Jn.6:35
He called His bread:
  "**The bread of truth**," Jn.6:32
    "**The bread of God**," v.33
      "**The bread of life**:"

We, like His disciples pray,
"Lord, evermore give us this Bread." v.34

The bread was only eaten by the priests. Lev.24:9:
1 Sam.21:1-6; Mt.12:4; 1 Pet.2:9; Rev.1:6; 5:10
We are the priesthood of believers that eat the Bread of Life.

The Body of Christ is one Bread. 1 Cor.10:17
"We being many are one bread, and one body: for we are all partakers of that one bread."
Christ is the children's Bread. Mk.7:27
For our healing and health.

**Border**, (crown)
speaks of our Security in Christ. Rom.8:34-39
The Word of God is "Forever Settled." Ps.119:89

His Church holds forth and exhibit the Bread of His Word.
We do not labor in vain. Phil.2:16
The revelation of the Bread (His Word) increases the quality and depth of our fellowship.

**Purpose**
The purpose of the Table was to display the Shewbread. Lev.24:5-9
Actually the consumption itself was an act of worship.
We seek a fresh supply of His Living Bread daily.
Mt.6:11; Jn.6:35

**Bread**, speaks of Nourishment.
(Means of sustaining life) 2 Cor.9:10

**Unleaven Bread**, is True Teaching. It is without false doctrine and sin.
Mt.26:17; Mk.14:1,12; Lk.22:15-22; Ac.12:3; 20:6; 1 Cor.5:7,8

**Leaven Bread**, is False Teaching. Decay, spiritual corruption and sin. Paul refers to it as malice and wickedness.
1 Cor.6-8; Mt.16:6,12; Mk.8:15; Lk.12:1; 13:21

**Crowns**
Two Crowns on this Table,
speak of Two Crowns for Christ
A Crown of Humility Mt.27:29; Prov.15:33
A Crown of Honor. Heb.2:9

**Vessels**
The vessels were the dishes, spoons, covers and the bowls. All made of pure gold. Ex.25:29
The dishes (chargers) were used to carry the bread into the Holy Place and for the placement of the bread. Setting the bread in order, speaks of the handling of God's Word.

The twelve Spoons were small cups that were filled with frankincense and burned on top of the bread. Lev.24:7; Num.7:14

**Ring**s, speak of "Daily in the temple, and in every house, they ceased not to teach and preach Jesus Christ. Ac.5:42

**Staves**, to carry His Word.
Mk.16:15 Jesus said,
"Go ye into all the world, and preach the gospel to every creature."

**Rings and Staves together**, continual teaching of His Word until Jesus returns.

The Lord's Supper is primarily a Love Feast to God and His Church. The Scriptures frequently picture the Lord teaching at the Table.

**The Table of Shewbread is:**
   **- symbol of Fellowship;**
      **- Food of God;**
         **- Feast of Love.**

The Coverings for the Table of Shewbread while on the march were:
1. A Num.4:7,8 cloth of Blue.
2. A cloth of Scarlet.
3. A covering of Badger's Skin.

# Chapter 6

**The Golden Altar, to burn incense.**

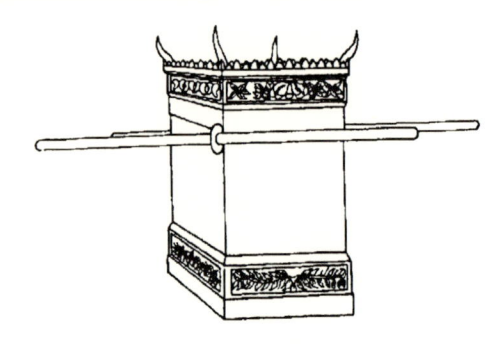

**Jesus ever lives to make intercession for us.**
Heb.7:25; Rom.8:34

Bible study outline No.6
1. **Visual illustration**.
   Golden Altar to burn Incense.
   Ex.30:1-7; 37:25-28
2. **Type of Christ**.
   Jesus is our Intercessor.
   Heb.7:25; Rom.8:34;
   Jn.17:1-26
3. **Applied to the believer**.
   Jesus our advocate with the Father.
   1 Jn.2:1; Heb.9:24
4. **Believer's responsibility**.
   Pray without ceasing.
   1 Thess.5:17

It was called:
Altar to Burn Incense. Ex.30:1
   (Reveals its purpose)
Incense Altar. Ex.35:15; 37:25
   (Only Incense was burned on it)
Golden Altar. Ex.39:38; 40:26; Num.4:11
   (Divine Nature of the Truth).
Altar of Sweet Incense before the Lord.
   Lev.4:7
Altar before the Lord. Lev.16:12,18; 4:7,18
   (Before the Lord)
Whole Altar that is by the Oracle.
   1 Kgs.6:22 (Makes us whole)
Golden Altar which is before the Throne.
   Rev.8:3 (For rulers)

**Physical Characteristics** Ex.30:1-10; 37:25-29
The Golden Altar 1 ½ ft. sq., 3 ft. high. It was made of shittim wood overlaid with pure gold. The Altar was 18 ins. Sq. It had a horn on each of the corners, wood overlaid with gold It had a crown of gold round about it, two golden rings under it's crown by the two corners thereof, upon the two sides for the two staves to bear it. The staves were made of shittim wood overlaid with gold.

**Size**
The Golden Altar was 3 feet high. The highest piece of furniture in the Holy Place,
speaks of The Father raised Jesus from the dead and set Him "Far **Above All." Jesus is head over all His Church.**
   Eph.1:20,21

"Which He wrought in Christ, when He raised Him from the dead, and set Him at His Own Right Hand in the heavenly place, far above all principality, and power, and might, and dominion, and every name that is named, not only in this world, but also in that which is to come:"

**Material**
The Golden Altar was made of shittim wood overlaid completely with pure gold.

**Pure Gold**, speaks of His Divine Nature.
**Wood**, speaks of His Perfect Humanity.

**Rings**
The Altar had two rings of gold under the crown by the two corners for the staves to bare it,
speak of Christ's Unending Prayer for us:
Heb.7:25
Jesus, "Ever lives to make intercession."

This applies to the believer's unending prayer.

To pray without ceasing. 1 Thes.5:17

Men ought always to pray. Lk.18:1; 21:36

The disciples said, "Lord, teach us to pray." Lk.11:1

Large or long prayers do not many times avail much, but the simple prayer of faith does from a pure heart.

Jas.5:16
"The effectual fervent prayer of a righteousness man avails much."

**Staves**
The Altar had two staves of shittim wood overlaid with gold, speak of Movement and Mobility.
Jesus prayed everywhere He went. He is our example of prayer.

We "Pray every where, lifting up holy hands, without wrath and doubting." 1 Tim. 2:8

**The Rings and Staves Together,**
speak of His Continual Prayer and Intercession at the right hand of the Father. Ac.2:33
Jesus has a Continual Personal Presence with us:
In Mt.28:20 Jesus said,
"I AM with you always, even unto the end of the world. Amen."

**Horns**
The Altar had four horns on the top pointing outward and upward towards the four corners of the earth.

The horns on the Brazen Altar, speak of the power in His Blood.

The horns here on the Golden Altar,
speaks of Jesus in His power in prayer.
Jesus demonstrated the power of prayer and intercession.
Jn.17:1-26

He is at the right hand of God and has all power. Mt.28:18-20

There is power and strength in His intercession to bring us into the fullness of God. This is the strength of the believer:
We have power in His Blood. We have power in prayer.
A perfect refuge in prayer. Heb.4:16

The Golden Altar applied to the believer is the place where we live in the expectation of God's power and answered prayer.

**Purpose**
The Fire for the Golden Altar were the Live Coals taken from the Brazen Altar.
It was an Altar exclusively to burn Incense. Ex.30:9

Only the priests could minister at the Golden Altar.
Ex.30:7,8; Num.4:16; Deut.33:10; 1 Sam.2:28;
1 Chron.6:49; 2 Chron.2:4; 13:11

The priests burned sweet incense on this Altar twice daily, every morning and evening as an act of worship to the Lord. Ex.30:7,8

The morning incense was offered at the third hour (9 a.m.) and the evening incense at the ninth hour (3 p.m.). Incense was burned at the same time the oil in the Candlestick was replenished and the daily burnt-offering was made. Num.28:3,4

1 Tim.2:8; Jn.4:21,23
We have a continuing praying spirit about us to
"Pray always, with all prayer and supplication in the Spirit, and watching thereunto with all perseverance and supplication for all saints."

Eph.6:18
"Continue in prayer, and watch in the same with thanksgiving."
Col.4:2
"Continuing instant in prayer." Rom.12:12
Our access into the Holiest (Presence of God) is always open through prayer.

Jesus lived a life of sacrifice and praise unto His Father. It also applies to us. Heb.13:15
"By Him therefore let us offer the sacrifice of praise to God continually, that is, the fruit of our lips giving thanks to His name."

The Blood of Jesus our sin-offering is the basis of His intercession at the right hand of the Father.

The blood on the horns of the Golden Altar. Lev.16:18,19; 4:7,18 speak of the power of His Blood in prayer.

We come, "boldly unto the throne of grace, that we may obtain mercy, and find grace to help in time of need, because we have been accepted in our beloved Christ. Heb.4:16; 1 Jn.1:7; 2:1

Incense Ex.30:34-38
Speaks of Jesus our Sweet Smelling Savor.
Eph.5:2
"Walk in love, as Christ also hath loved us, and hath given Him self for us an offering and a sacrifice to God for a sweet smelling savor." 2 Cor.2:15; Phil.4:18

To burn incense means to pray.
Rev.5:8
"Golden vials full of odors, which are the prayers of saints."

**Incense**,
is a type of the true prayers of believers through Christ.
Ps.141:2
"Let my prayer be set forth before thee as incense;"

Rev.8:3, 4
"Another angel came and stood at the altar, having a golden censer; and there was given unto him much incense, that he should offer it with the prayers of all saints upon the golden sltar which was before the throne." And the smoke of the incense, which came with the prayers of the saints, ascended up before God out of the angel's hand."

The pure sweet incense of sweet spices was composed of
four ingredients
Ex.30:34-38
  - Stacte, speaks of His Life.
  - Onycha, speaks of His Death.
  - Galbanum, speaks of His Resurrection.
  - Frankincense, speaks of His Ascension.

The Ingredients, that made up the incense,
speaks of the Holy Spirit of God upon Jesus.
Typifies the work of the Holy Spirit in the Life of Christ.

Mt.3:16
"Jesus when He was baptized, went up straightway out of
  the water: and, lo, the heavens were opened unto Him, and
  He saw the Spirit of God descending like a dove and
  lighting upon Him:" Isa.42:1; Mt.3:16; Mt.12:18

Jesus is the perfume of God. All worship must be through Jesus
who has passed into the Holiest, having obtained eternal
redemption for us. Heb.9:12

The perfume of the believer is:
**Prayer**, to pray without ceasing. To maintain a Spirit of Prayer.
**Praise and Worship**, first by living the life of Christ.
**In the Spirit**, by being influenced, led and directed by the Holy
Spirit.
**With the Freedom of the Spirit**, in the pure truth of God's
Word.
2 Cor.3:17
"Now the Lord is that Spirit: and where the Spirit of the Lord
  is, there is liberty." (Freedom)

Where the truth is preached the Holy Spirit will convict the hearts of men and souls will be saved. Grace will abound. This is how we perfume the Sanctuary.

**Censer**
The golden vessel that held the Fire,
speaks of the Holiness of God. It was full.
Heb.9:4; Rev.8:3,5; 1 Kgs.7:50

A type of Christ. Jesus is the Holiness of God. He is full.
Jesus is the Holy One of Israel. Mighty in Holiness.
Ac.2:27; 3:14

It speaks to us the believer,
"without holiness no man shall see God." Heb.12:14

**Crown**
The Altar had a Crown of gold around the top which kept the Fire and the incense from falling on to the ground.
The Golden Crown,
speaks of Jesus is the resurrected and exalted one seated on the right hand of the Father.
We may now expect the power of answered prayer.

**Location**
The Golden Altar was located in the Holy Place on the east side before the Inner Veil. Ex.30:6; 40:26
Through prayer we enter into the presence of God through the Flesh (Blood) of Christ.

Directions for removing the Golden Altar. Num.4:14; Num.4:11,12
When on the march the Golden Altar was covered with:
1. A cloth of blue.
2. A badger's skin.

Chapter 7

**The Candlestick, speaks of Light and Testimony.**

**Jesus said, "I AM, the Light of the world." Jn.8:12**

Bible study outline No.7
1. **Visual illustration.**
   Golden Candlestick. Ex.25:31-39; 37:17:24
2. **Type of Christ.**
   Jesus is the Light of the world. Jn.8:12; 9:5; 1:4,5,9
3. **Applied to the believer.**
   Receive the Light. Jn.3:21; 1 Thess.5:5
4. **Believer's responsibility.**
   We are His lights to the world.
   Mt.5:14-16; Jn.12:35,36; Rev.1:12-20

   a. **Walk in the Light.** 1 Jn.1:7; Eph.5:8; Ps.119:105

   b. **Shine as lights in the world.** Phil.2:15; Isa.60:1

   c. **Keep the lights burning.** Lk.12:35,36

It was called:
- Candlestick. Ex.25:31; 37:17
- Pure Candlestick. Lev.24:4
  (Lampstand or Light bearer

**Physical Characteristics** Ex.25:31-40; 37:17-24
The Candlestick was made of one talent of pure gold. The main vine was the actual "Candlestick" or better the "Body of Christ." The main vine had four knobs, four flowers and six branches made with a decoration of the almond, bud and flower. It had three branches on each side of the main vine. Three bowls made like unto almonds, with a knob and a flower in one each of the six branches.
Upon each of the branches rested a source of light. A bowl of olive oil and a wick. It gave the appearance of an almond bush. It had snuffers of gold, tongs to trim the wicks and snuff dishes to hold the trimmings.

**Size**
God gave no measurements for the Candlestick.
There is no end to His Light in us. 2 Cor.4:6
The light we receive of Him is eternal. Jn.3:16
A light to shine before the Lord from glory to glory. 2 Cor.3:18

**Material**
The Candlestick was made of pure gold. Hand beaten into a Lamp stand. One piece of a beaten work into shape without seam.

When Jesus said, God was His Father the Jews sought to kill Him, because they said He made Himself equal with God. Jn.5:18

Who, being in the form of God, thought it not robbery to be equal with God: Phil.2:6

Jesus came to make known His Father. When He did conviction was brought upon men. They got mad at God and took it out on Jesus.

When we minister His Word, conviction falls upon the hearts of people. They get mad at Jesus and take it out on us.

God is working out the seams in our life. He is perfecting us. The more the shaping we receive, the bigger His Testimony in our lives.

After our cleansing at Calvary we have become new creatures in Christ. 2 Cor.5:17  God begins to shape us, form us and to make us into the very image of His only begotten son.
Rom.8:29; 2 Pet.1:4; 3:18; Heb.12:10; Eph.5:26, 27

The Holy Spirit molds us so that our outer fleshly tabernacle confirms to the inner man. We are being transformed into the very image and fashion of God! 2 Cor.3:18

**Located**
Candlestick was located in the Holy Place on the south side.
Ex.26:35; 40:22,24,26; Heb.9:2,6
The Holy Place was completely dark without the light of the Candlestick. It was the only light in the Holy Place.

We are in complete darkness without Jesus. He is the only true source of Spiritual Light in His Church.

By the power of the Holy Spirit He dwells in us and lights up His Church. We are His lights that shine in this present evil dark world.
Phil.2:15 "Ye shine as lights in the world;"

**The Candlestick is light by day and night**.
The lamps were dressed in the morning and in the evening with new oil. Ex.30:7,8; Ps.92:10

The priests would trim the wicks and fill the lamps with the purest olive oil. Ex.27:20,21; Lev.24:1-4

It was the priests responsibility to light the lamps in the Holy Place. Ex.27:20; Lev.24:4; 1 Sam.3:3
It gave light for them as they went about their service. Ex.27:21; Lev.24:3,4

They were responsible for cleaning, filling and lighting the lamps. The lamps were to "Burn Continually." Lev.24:2; Ex.27:20

It is our responsibility to be filled with the Holy Spirit. We know without God's Light which is Christ in us, we can do nothing. We cannot serve, give direction to others nor lead souls to Christ.

Do we cry out in the morning and evening hours, "Lord give me oil, fill my lamp." So, we may be ready in the midnight hour.

Remember the ten virgins in Mt.25:1-13
Five were wise and five were foolish. Thank God we are like the five wise virgins who kept their (vessels) lamps filled with oil. Lk.12:35
Jesus is Coming Soon.

The Candlestick was the only light in the Holy Place.
**There were three lights in the Tabernacle**:
1. Natural light of the sun in the Outer Court.
2. Light from the Candlestick in the Holy Place.
3. Light of the Shekinah Glory in the Holy of Holies

**Purpose**
The Candlestick gave light for the priests to serve in the Holy Place.
Jesus is our light to serve for the greater the works He said we would do.
Jn.14:12
"I say unto you, He that believeth on me, the works that I do shall he do also; and greater works than these shall he do; because I go unto my Father."

Greater works in quanity not greater in quality. We do these greater works through Him by the power of the Holy Spirit.

Jesus, is free from sin. Mighty in holiness. Pure and kind is the True Lamp of God. Through Him we are free from sin, mighty in holiness, pure and kind.
Jn.8:32-36; Rom.6:18,22; Gal.5:1,13

"**Pure Candlestick**." Ex.31:8; Lev.24:1-4
Pure light fueled it with pure olive oil called
"**Pure Golden Oil**."
Jesus is the Pure Candlestick.

God called for the lamps. He arranged them in His order on the Candlestick.
The six lamps are a type of believers. We are called by God. He has set us in order in His Church.

On the top of each of the six branches was a wick and a bowl of pure olive oil. Upon each branch rested a source of light:

The **wicks,** connected the oil supply.
They speak of the lives of believers. We keep our lives clean with a fresh supply of oil. The pureness of the Holy Spirit to keep our light burning bright.

The wicks were trimmed and clean. If we keep our lives clean then we will burn with a bright light.
Jesus cleans up our lives with daily reading and study of His Word. Our lives do not gather dirt and soot. His Flame does not flicker, but continues to burn bright.

There were three branches on each side of the Candlestick.
Three, speaks of Divine Testimony.
God, the Father promised us His Light.
God, the Son, the Lord Jesus Christ is the Light.
God, the Holy Spirit Reveals the Light
 We are witnesses to His Light.

**Seven lamps on top held the oil**. They were fashioned like almonds. The almond tree is the first tree to bare it's fruit in the spring. Almonds speak of Resurrection. 1 Cor.15:20-23

Jesus said, "I AM the resurrection," Jn.11:25
Christ, the resurrection of the First-fruits,
speaks of the Holy Spirit resurrecting us into newness of life.

In the resurrection power of Christ through the Holy Spirit we have received the new birth. We are new creatures in Him with a new heart and a new mind.
Rom.6:4; 12:2; Eph.4:23; 2 Cor.5:17
Our newness of life is living above sin in this present evil world.

The **Flame**, speaks of believers Burning Brightly under the influence, direction and living by the power of the Holy Spirit. Always being used by God and giving Him all the glory.
We are filled with His Spirit, live by His Spirit, walk in His Spirit and are led by His Spirit. We are the true testimony of Christ, because He lives in us.
Heb.1:7 He makes, "His ministers a flame of fire." Ps.104:4

**Oil**, is a type of the Holy Spirit. Jesus is God's Anointed One.
These lamps were filled with oil,
speaks of the believer's being filled with the Holy Spirit.

The knops, speak of His Fruitfulness.
Jesus is God's Perfect Fruit Bearer. He said, Jn.15:1,
"I AM the True Vine, and My Father is the Husbandman."

v.5, "I AM the Vine, ye are the branches: He that abides in Me, and I in him, the same brings forth much fruit: for without Me ye can do nothing."

v.8, "Herein is My Father glorified, that ye bear much fruit; so shall ye be My disciples."

We bear fruit through Jesus. Gal.5:22,23
"The fruit of the Spirit is love, joy, peace, longsuffering,
  gentleness, goodness, faith, Meekness, temperance:."

Jesus abides in us and we in Him. We are connected to the Main Vine. We bring forth much fruit. Jn.15:4,5; Col.1:6

Jesus is the Main Vine. We are the branches. We can only be His fruit bearers by being connected to Him.

The **Flowers** were fashioned after the almond tree.
Almond blossoms for beauty, fragrance and Glory.
Speak of the light and pure, holy life of Christ.

**Flowers,** also speak of His Beauty and Glory.
We have received His resurrected life and light.
We live a pure, holy life in Christ.

The Golden Candlestick was made of one piece.
God sees us in Christ. The light of the lamps all merged into one great light. A unity of purpose with no competition.

---

Seven lamps burning brightly.
**Seven**, speaks of Divine Perfection; Completeness.
The fullness of God for the believer. We are perfected and completed in Christ. Col.2:10; 4:12

**Seven times Jesus announced His Return in the book of Revelation.** 2:25; 3:3, 11; 16:15; 22:7, 12, 20
There are seven "**Blessed**" in this book
Rev.1:3; 14:13; 16:15; 20:6; 22:7, 14
Blessed are they which are called unto the "Marriage Supper of the Lamb."

**Seven-fold Spirit on Christ.** Isa.11:1,2
"There are seven lamps of fire burning before
  the throne, which are the seven Spirits of God." Rev.4:5

**Seven I AM'S of Jesus in the Gospel of John**.
Jn.6:35; .8:12; 10:9; 10:11; 11:25; 14:6; Jn.15:1

**Seven words of Christ from the Cross**:
Lk.23:34; Lk.23:43; Jn.19:26-27 'Mt.27:46; Mk.15:34'
Jn.19:28; Jn.19:30; Lk.23:46

**"There are seven lamps of fire burning before the throne,
  which are the seven Spirits of God."** Rev.4:5

**Seven-fold Ministry of the Holy Spirit:**
1. The Spirit of Grace. Heb.10:29
2. The Spirit of Grace, Supplication and Prayer. Zech.12:10; Rom.8:26; Eph.6:18
3. The Spirit of Adoption. Rom.8:15
4. The Spirit of Glory. 1 Pet.4:14
5. The Spirit of Holiness. Rom.1:4
6. The Spirit of Life in Christ Jesus. Rom.8:2
7. The Spirit of Truth. Jn.16:13
   One Spirit. The Holy Spirit in His seven-fold ministry at work in His Church.

**The Seven-fold Spirit on Christ.**
Isa.11:2
"The **Spirit of the Lord** shall rest upon Him. (Jesus) the **Spirit of Wisdom** and **Understanding**, the **Spirit of Counsel** and **Might**, the **Spirit of Knowledge** and of the **Fear of the Lord**;"

The book of Revelation contains many "Seven's."
7 Spirits before the throne.
7 Stars in Christ's right hand.
Jesus is walking in the midst of 7 golden Candlesticks.
7 letters to the Churches of Asia.
The book is sealed with 7 seals.
7 angels standing before the throne.
7 trumpets.
7 vials of judgments.
7 thunders utter their voices. etc.

The number seven appears nearly 600 times throughout the Bible (in types).

**The Holy Anointing Oil.** Ex.30:23-25; 37:29
Is a type of the Holy Spirit, speaks of Christ the Anointed.
In Lk.4:18,19 Jesus said,
"The Spirit of the Lord is upon Me, because He hath anointed me to preach the gospel to the poor; He hath sent me to heal the brokenhearted, to preach deliverance to the captives, and recovering of sight to the blind, to set at liberty them that are bruised, To preach the acceptable year of the Lord.
This prophecy is spoken from Isa.61:1-3
It is fulfilled by Jesus. Ac.10:38; Heb.1:9; Ps.45:17

In Ac.10:38
"How God anointed Jesus of Nazareth with the Holy Spirit and with power: who went about doing good and healing all that were oppressed of the devil; for God was with Him."

**Principles spices of the Holy Anointing Oil.**
Ex.30:23-25; 37:39
a. **Pure Myrrh**, speaks of the outward pouring of Christ's Love to redeem us.
b. **Sweet Cinnamon**, speaks of His Holy jealously for the honor and glory of God. Jesus always had that burning zeal.
c. **Sweet Calamus**, speaks of His upright and righteousness. His witness to the truth.
d. **Cassia,** speaks of His submission to and worship of God. Jesus was spontaneous in worship.
e. **Oil Olive**, is a type of the Holy Spirit. Christ is the Anointed One. Jesus is the living witness unto perfection. His love flows literally free, willing and at liberty!

There were nine ingredients in the sweet incense and holy anointing oil. Ex.30:23,24-26

The value of the Golden Candlestick is found in the richness in Christ.

**Direction for removing the Candlestick**
Num.4:9,10
1. The Candlestick was wrapped in a blue cloth.
2. Upon the blue cloth it was wrapped in Badger's skin.

**The priest, and his garments of glory and beauty in the Holy Place.**

Heb.8:1
**"We have such an high priest, who is set on the right hand of the throne of the Majesty in the heavens;"**
Heb.10:12; 12:2; Eph.1:20; Col.3:1

...can you imagine the high priest going about his daily service in the Holy Place, arranging the bread on the Table, burning the sweet Incense, and dressing the Lamps.
The golden bells on the hem of his robe, sent up a glorious sound that he was about his Father's business!

… and then suddenly! God, Himself rent the veil in two when Jesus died upon the Cross for our sins.
(This took place in the temple. Jn.2:20-22; Mt.27:51,52)

**The Holy Place, is a type of His Church.** Ac.7:38

1. At the Table of Shewbread,
    Jesus is the Bread of Life. Jn.6:35
        We eat the bread of life.
            Jn.6:32-58; 1 Cor.10:17

2. At the Golden Altar of Incense,
    Jesus is our Intercessor.
        Heb.7:25; Rom.8:34; Jn.17:1-26
            We burn incense, which means to pray
            for one another without ceasing.
                1 Thess.5:17; Eph.6:18; Rom.1:9; Lk.18:1

3. At the Golden Candlestick.
    Jesus is the Light of the world.
        Jn.8:12; Mt.4:16
            We contain and reflect the light of Christ.
                Mt.5:14; Phil.2:15; Isa.60:1

The priest served in the Holy Place: tasted the bread, smelled the incense and saw the light.

**God's design for us in His church:**
To be God's beloved people in whom He is well pleased.
Jesus tells us today who serve in His Church to:
- Eat the Bread of Life, (which is Christ)
- Burn the Incense, (which means to pray) and
- contain His Light of Christ by the power of the Holy Spirit.
  **To Eat, Pray and then Shine!**

**Our responsibility in His Church is to:**
- Keep His Table Set (Feast upon His Word)
- Keep the Spirit of Prayer alive and
- His Light Burning Bright within us.

Example:
Jesus, went about teaching His Word. Preaching the Gospel of the kingdom and healing all manner of sickness and all manner of disease among the people. Mt.4:23

# Chapter 8

The Veil _____

**Holy of Holies, represents God's Special Dwelling Place on earth in the midst of His people.** Ex.25:22; Num.7:89

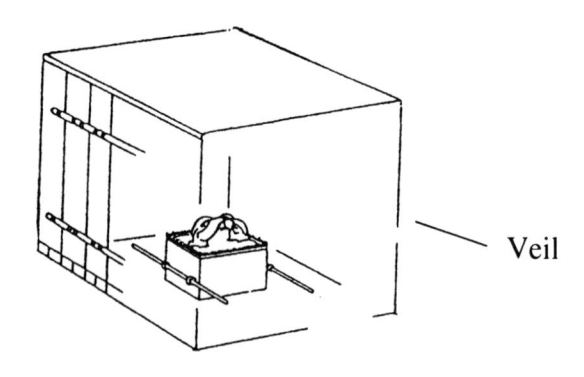

Veil

**The Holy of Holies is a type of the third Heaven. God's Throne Room.** Heb.9:24; 6:19,20; 9:12,24; 10:19

**God Dwells in us through Christ by the power of the Holy Spirit.**
Rom.8:9-16; 1 Jn.4:13; 3:24

The Holy of Holies contained two pieces
of furniture which formed one piece:
1. The Ark (of the Covenant).
2. The Mercy Seat, with two Cherubim.
   Ex.26:33,34; Heb.9:3-7

It was called:
- Most Holy Place. Ex.26:34
 - Holiest of all. Heb.9:3
 - Holy Place. Heb.9:12,24
 - Holiest. Heb.10:19
 - Second Tabernacle. Heb.9:7
 - Third Heaven. 2 Cor.12:2

The Holy of Holies was located at the west end of the Tabernacle Proper. It was 15 ft. long 15 ft. wide and 15 ft. high. The Holy of Holies was a perfect cube, 10x10x10 cubits, 15x15x15 ft.)
The Holy City (New Jerusalem) is a perfect cube, 1500x1500x1500

---

**Veil, speaks of the Flesh (blood) of Christ.** Heb.10:19,20; 9:12; 6:19,20

**We enter now into the Presence of God through the Flesh (Blood) of Christ.** Heb.10:19,20

Bible study outline No.8
1. **Visual illustration**.
   Veil. Ex.26:31-33; 36:35,36
2. **Type of Christ**.
   The Flesh of Jesus Christ. Heb.10:19,20
   His Humanity was the Veil of the Godhead.
   Ac.17:29; Rom.1:20; Col.2:9
   Jesus is our way into the Presence of God.
   Jn.14:6; 2 Cor.3:4; 1 Tim.2:5
   The Veil was rent. Mt.27:51; Lk.23:45; Mk.15:38
3. **Applied to the believer**.
   We have entered into the Presence of God through the Flesh of Christ. Heb.6:19,20; 7:25; 9:3-12
4. **Believer's responsibility**.
   Come boldly before the Throne of God. Heb.4:16
   Live in the Presence of God.

It was called:
1. Veil (or Veil in the New Testament).
   Ex.26:31; Heb.6:19 (a divider)).
2. Second Veil. Heb.9:3
   of the actual Tabernacle building the Door being the "First Veil."
3. Covering Veil. Num.4:5
   It covered the Ark when the camp moved.
4. Veil of the Covering. Ex.35:12; 39:34; 40:21
5. The Veil of the Testimony. Lev.24:3
   It covered the Tables of the Law which were inside the Ark.
6. The Veil of the Sanctuary. Lev.4:6
   Inside the Sanctuary, it divided the Priest from the Holy of Holies.

The Heb. Word for "Veil" means "a screen, separator, Curtain; that which hides."
The Veil divided the Holy of Holies from the Holy place.
It served as a barrier between the two rooms.

**Physical characteristics**
The Veil was 15 ft. wide and high. It was made of fine twined linen of white, blue, purple, scarlet with Cherubim.

It was suspended by gold rings from four pillars of shittim wood overlaid with gold with four sockets of silver at their bases. Ex.26:31-33; 36:35,36; 40:41

The Veil was made of "Cunning work." The Heb. Word for "Cunning" means "The work of a thinker."

**The Colors of the Veil were**:
**White**, speaks of His Holiness.
Heb.7:26 "Jesus a high priest became us, who is holy, harmless, undefiled, separate, from sinners, and made higher than the heavens;"
Jesus dwells within us, we have access to His Holiness!
Heb.4:15
We live a holy life! Heb.12:14; Rev.19:7-9.
**Blue**, speaks of Jesus in Heaven.
Heb.4:14; 9:24; 1 Tim.3:16
**Purple**, speaks of Jesus at the Throne of God. Rom.8:34
**Scarlet**, speaks of Jesus completed His Sacrifice
Atonement and Suffering. He is now at the right hand of the Father. Heb.10:12
**Cherubim**, speak of Jesus the Guardian of our way in Holiness.
Eph.5:26 The Veil was made of fine twined linen.

**Size**
The veil was 15 ft. wide and 15 ft. high. This Veil was the only entrance into the Holy of Holies.
Only the high priest could enter in through the Veil once a year on the Day of Atonement. Lev.16:29; 23:27-31; Num.29:7

**Material**
The material of the Veil was made of fine twined linen.
Fine Linen, speaks of His Holiness.

**Location**
The Veil hung between the Holy Place and the Holy of Holies.

**Purpose**
It served as a barrier to keep everyone out of the Holy Presence of God,
speaks of the Flesh of Christ. Heb.10:19,20.
His Humanity was the Veil of the Godhead.
Ac.17:29; Rom.1:20; Col.2:9

When Jesus died for our sins on the Cross of Calvary God rent the Veil from top to bottom (tore in two pieces)
Mt.27:50; Lk.23:44-46; Mk.15:37, 38; Heb.9:12; 6:19,20; Jn.14:6

The Veil was rent by God, not by man.
Mt.27:51; Lk.23:45; Mk.15:38
The Veil was to high. No human hand could reach it.
(God rent the Veil in the midst in the Temple).

This ended the earthly priesthood. Jesus is our only Great High Priest. Heb.7:26; 9:11; 2 Tim.2:5

Jesus is our only way into the Presence of God.
Heb.10:19,20
"Having therefore, brethren, boldness to enter into the holiest by the blood of Jesus, by a new and living way, which He (Jesus) hath consecrated for us, through the veil, that is to say, His Flesh;" 9:12; Jn.14:6

We now have direct access to God through Christ. There is no longer a wall separating us from God.
Eph.2:14
"He (Jesus) is our peace, who hath made both one, and hath broken down the middle wall of partition between us;"

The Veil Rent,
speaks of the Completeness of Christ's Sacrifice.
Jesus on the Cross of Calvary said, "It is finished." Jn.19:30

The Veil was rent to bring us to God. 1 Pet.3:18
Jesus fulfilled the Whole Law. Mt.5:17 Jesus did what the Law could not do.
Rom.8:2,3
"For the law of the Spirit of life in Christ Jesus hath made me free from the law of sin and death. For what the law could not do, in that it was weak through the flesh, God sending His Own Son in the likeness of sinful flesh, and for sin, condemned sin in the flesh:" Heb.10:20; 9:8

The Veil in Heaven is Now Open through the Blood of Jesus, because He made an Atonement for our souls.
Rev.11:19; 15:5; Heb.10:12

**Veil Pillars, speak of Jesus was " Cut off" in the midst of His days for our sins.**

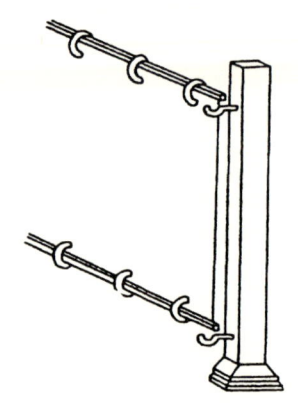

**We are cut off, Separated from this evil world to Serve God in holiness.**

The four pillars were without chapiters. They were cut off and uncrowned.
Speak of Jesus, "Was cut off out of the land of the living: for the transgression of My people was He Stricken." Isa.53:8 Punished (Ps.102:23,24

Jesus was cut off from us, because of our sins. He made an Atonement for us so we may receive forgiveness from our sins.

The four pillars upholding the veil were made of shitim wood overlaid with gold set in silver sockets.

The veil hung from gold hooks connected to the pillars or from a screen squared on four completed bars. Ex.26:32; 36:36

These four pillars, speak of Jesus in a fourfold
perfection meeting our fourfold need.
Jesus is to us:
1. Wisdom.
2. Righteousness.
3. Sanctification.
4. Redemption.
    1 Cor.1:30

Their four silver sockets formed the base for the pillars.
The silver was taken from the redemption money.
We have been redeemed with His Precious Blood of Christ
to serve and worship Him. To live in the presence of God.

The Hooks were gold upon which the veil hung
(Hooks from above). Ex.26:32; 36:36
Speaks of Jesus was sustained and supported from on high
while He was here on earth.
We are sustained and supported from on high through Christ
by the power of the Holy Spirit

# Chapter 9

**The Ark, speaks of the Person of Christ:**
**Gold, speaks of Jesus Perfect God.**
**Wood, speaks of Jesus Perfect Man.**

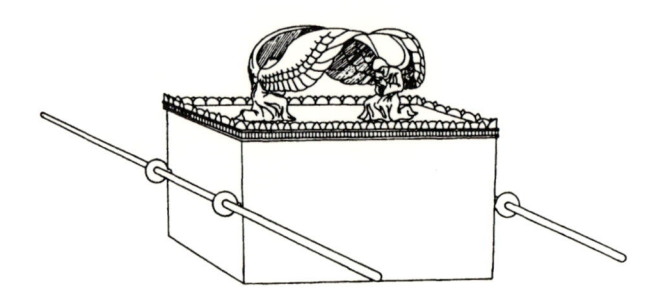

**Jesus is not only the Son of God, but in Spirit He is God!**

"Unto us a Child is born, unto us a Son is given: and the government shall be upon His shoulder: and His Name shall be called wonderful, counselor, the mighty God, the everlasting Father, the prince of peace." Isa.9:6

**Jesus, "Is the image of the invisible God" Col. 1:15**

Bible study outline No.9
1. **Visual illustration**.
    Ark. Ex.25:10-25; 37:1-5
2. **Type of Christ**.
    a  Jesus, Divine Son of God.
        1 Tim.3:16; Rom.8:3; Jn.1:1,14; Phil..2:6,7
    b. Everlasting Blood Covenant.
        Heb.13:20; Mt.26:28; Mk.14:24; Lk.22:20
3. **Applied to the believer**.
    We are partakers of His Divine Nature through faith in His Blood. 2 Pet.1:4
    Receive His Divine Nature. Jn.3:5,6; 5:24; 2 Cor.5:17
4. **Believer's responsibility**.
    Live under His Everlasting Blood Covenant by faith in His Blood. Rom.3:25; 6:12,18; 8:16

It was called:
1. Ark of shittim wood. Ex.25:10
   (Fulness of the Godhead Bodily)
2. Ark of the Testimony. Ex.25:22; 30:6;
   Num.7:89 (Witness of God)
3. Ark of the Covenant of the Lord.
   Num.10:33 (Relationship with God)
4. Ark of the Covenant of the Lord of all the earth. Josh.3:11 (Over all enemies)
5. Ark of God. 1 Sam.3:3 (Victory is His alone)
6. Holy Ark. 2 Chron.35:3 (Holiness of God)
7. Ark of Thy Strength. 2 Chron.6:41;
   Ps.132:8  (Strength of God)
8. Ark of the Lord. Josh.4:11 (He is Lord)
9. Ark of the God of Israel. 1 Sam.5:7
   (For His people)
10. Ark of the Lord, the Lord of all the earth.
    Josh.3:13 (All enemies)
11. Ark of the Covenant of God. Judg.20:27
12. Ark of the Lord God. 1 Kgs.2:26

**Physical** Characteristics Ex.25:10-15; 37:1-5
The Ark was made of shittim wood 3 ft. 9 ins. long 2 ft. 3 ins. wide and high. The Ark was overlaid with pure gold, within and without. It had a crown of gold round about it on the top. Four rings of gold in the four corners. Two rings on each side in which two staves of shittim wood overlaid with gold were inserted. One stave on each side in the rings. The staves were in the rings and were not taken from it.

**Size**
The Ark was 3 ft 9 ins long, 2 ft. 3 ins. wide and 2 ft. 3 ins. high. Moses saw only part of the Glory of God and his face shined so bright that he had to ware a veil over his face when he came before the congregation of the people.

Jesus is the Shekinah Glory. Jn.17:5
He dwells in us now, by the power of the Holy Spirit. We have full access to God's Glory through Him.


**Material**
The Ark was made of shittim wood overlaid with pure gold within and without, speaks of the Person of Christ in His two-fold Nature.

**Pure Gold**, speaks of Jesus Perfect God. Jn.1:1,14

**Wood**, speaks of Jesus Perfect Man. Heb.2:14

Only the gold on the Ark was visible to the eye, Yet, many people today only see His Human Nature, not His Divine Nature.
Born again believers see His Divine Nature.

We are partakers of His Divine Nature. When we see Him face to face then we shall be like Him for we shall see Him as He is.
1 Jn.3:2; (Rom.8:29, 30; Col.1:15-22)

**Rings**, (unending) speak of moving closer and closer to the fullness of God. Our revelation of Christ and His victory, mercy, lordship and truths are ever increasing in our life.

Two **Staves**, were not taken from the rings in the Ark, speaks to carry the pure truth of God's word that Jesus is divine to the world.

**Rings and staves together,**
To declare that Jesus is divine, the fullness of God and the basis of His Truth.

1. "Inspiration of the Scriptures."
    2 Tim.3:15-17; 1 Thess.2:13; 2 Pet.1:21
2. "Incarnation" God made Flesh.
    Mt.28:19; Lk.3:22
3. "Virgin Birth"
    Mt.1:23; Lk.1:31,35
4. "Blood Atonement"
    Lev.17:11; Heb.9:22; Jn.1:29,36;
    Mt.26:28 1 Cor.15:3; 2 Cor.5:21
5. "Resurrection of Jesus Christ"
    Mt.28:6; Lk.24:39; 1 Cor.15:4

**Location**
The Ark was located in the Presence of God.
Ex.25:22; Num.7:89
It was placed in the Holy of Holies behind the Veil on the west end of the Tabernacle Proper.
Ex.26:33; 40:21; Heb.9:3,4

Jesus is located in the Presence of God. Jn.1:18

We are in the Presence of God through Christ all the time.
Rom.8:1; 2 Cor.5:17

**Crown**
The Ark had a Crown of gold round about it.
Three pieces of furniture were crowned in the Tabernacle: the Ark, Golden Altar and Table of Shewbread.
A **crown,** speaks of the Kingship of Christ. Heb.2:9; 7:1,2

**Purpose**
The Ark (of the Covenant) contained God's Law, because the Ark was made for the Law. Ex.25:16

God had a blood covenant with the nation of Israel. Blood applied, speaks of the blood of Jesus is the Blood of the Everlasting Covenant.
Heb.13:20
"Now the God of peace that brought again from the dead our Lord Jesus, that great shepherd of the sheep, through the blood of the everlasting covenant,"
Heb.13:12; Mt.26:28; Mk.14:24; Lk.22:20

The Israelites inquired of the Lord before the Ark.
Josh.7:6-9; Judg.20:27; 1 Chron.13:3
We inquire of the Lord now through Christ, are lead and directed by the power of the Holy Spirit.

The Israelites were protected by the Ark as long as they kept God's Commandments.

Because we keep God's Word. We live the Christ-like life in holiness. When we ask of Him we receive. God protects us from our enemies and from the evil one. 1 Jn.2:3-8; 3:22-24; 5:2,3

**Ark contained God's Covenant.**
**speaks of the Blood of Jesus is the Blood of the Everlasting New Covenant. Heb.13:20**

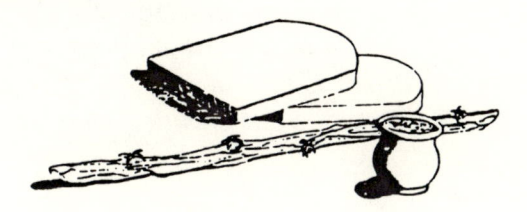

**Jesus said,**
**"This is my Blood of the new testament, which is shed for many for the remission of sins."** Mt.26:28

Contents of the Ark.
a. **Two Tables of the Law**. Ex.25:16; Deut.10:2,5
   Jesus is the Living Word. Jn.1:1,14
b. **A golden Pot of Manna**. Ex.16:32-34; Heb.9:4
   Jesus is our Spiritual. Jn.6:31-58; Rev.2:17
c. **Aaron's Rod that Budded**. Num.17:8-10; Heb.9:4
   Jesus is our Resurrection. Jn.11:25; 14:19

**The contents are typical of the Godhead.**
a. The Tables of the Law,
   the Father, the powerful lawgiver.
b. The golden pot of Manna,
   the Son, the Bread of Life.
c. The Rod that budded.
   The Holy Spirit, bearing fruit and life.

**Each item suggest a part of the three-fold nature of man:**
a. Law, speaks of God's provision for our soul.
b. Manna, speaks of His provision for our body.
c. Aaron's Rod that Budded, speaks of His provision for our spirit. (Resurrection and Newness of Life).

**To reflect on the Nature of God**
a. the Law, speaks of God and His Character.
b. the Manna, speaks of Christ our Spiritual Food.
c. Aaron's Rod that Budded, His resurrection and first fruits.

**Three articles are seen in Jn.14:6**
Jesus is:
a. The Way, the two Tables of the Law.
b. The Truth, the Golden Pot of Manna.
c. The Life, the Rod of Aaron that budded.

**A look at each item separately.**
Tables of the Law (Covenant). Heb.9:4
Israel had four aspects of the Law:
a. Moral Law.  b. Civil Law.  c. Ceremonial Law.
d. Health Laws.
God's Commandments were written on tables of stone in the Old Testament.
In the New Testament Jesus writes His
Commandments on the tables of our hearts.

**Manna in Heb. Means, "What is it?"
In Chalden it means, "It is a portion."**

It is called
a. God's Manna. Neh.9:20
b. Bread from Heaven. Ex.16:4
c. Bread of Heaven. Ps.105:40
d. Corn of Heaven. Ps.78:24
e. Angel's Food. Ps.78:25
f. Spiritual Meat. 1 Cor.10:3

**The Golden Pot of Manna. Heb.9:4**
a. Jesus is our, Bread from Heaven.
   (Bread of Life) Life Sustaining.
b. True Manna, Spiritual Food. Life Giving.
c. Complete Provision. Super-natural supply
   and All-sufficient Lord. Phil.4:19; Mt.6:11

Manna, speaks of life given. Jn.6:32,33
Shewbread, speaks of life sustained.
Josh.5:12; Jn.6:63; Rom.5:10

The Rod of Aaron that Budded.
   Heb.9:4; Num. Chs.12,16,17

**Aaron's Rod is a type of Christ:**
1. The Rod coming to Life,
   speaks of Christ's Resurrection.
2. The Rod Budded into an almond plant,
   speaks of Jesus the First-fruits from the dead
   1 Cor.15:20 and the Firstborn Son. Rom.8:29
   The Heb. Word for almond Is "Wakeful" or "Hastener."
3. The Rod Budded in the morning,
   speaks of Christ's Resurrection Morning, brought a New
   Day in God.

# Chapter 10

**Mercy Seat,
the blood of the sin offering was sprinkled upon it.**

**Jesus is our propitiation.
He pleads for our mercy before God.** Rom.3:24, 25


Bible study outline No.10
1. **Visual illustration.**
   Mercy Seat. Ex.25:17; 37:6
2. **Type of Christ.**
   Jesus is our Propitiation. (He pleads for our mercy before God).
   Rom.3:24,25; Heb.9:15; 9:12; 10:12; 7:25;
   1 Jn.4:10; 2:2; 1:1-3
3. **Applied to the believer.**
   To live in God's mercy through Christ.
   Heb.2:17; 4:14,16; Tit.3:5
4. **Believer's responsibility.**
   To proclaim God's mercy. Ac.13:38,39; Lk.6:36

It was called:
- Mercy Seat. Ex.25:17; 37:6
- Throne of God
- Throne of Glory.
- Jehovah's Throne upon the Ark.
- Throne of the Tabernacle.
    Place of Holiness, Justice and Righteousness.
    Atonement and Propitiation.
- Mercy and Reconciliation.
- Communion of God with redeemed man.
- The Glory of God.
- Where God recorded His Name. 2 Sam.6:1,2

God appeared upon the Mercy Seat in the form of His Shekinah Glory.

**Physical Characteristic.** Ex.25:17; 37:6
"Make a mercy seat of pure gold: 3 ft. 9 ins. long and 2 ft. 3 ins. wide.

**Size**
Ex.25:17-20; 37:6-9
The Mercy Seat was 3 ft. 9 ins. long 2 ft. 3 ins. wide.
God is the Eternal Spirit. Heb.9:14
"I am Alpha and Omega, the beginning and the end, the first and the last." Re 22:13

**Material**
The Mercy Seat was made of pure gold.
**Gold,** speaks of the Deity of Christ. He was pure.
Tried by God's Fire. To provide us a pure Atonement.

We are redeemed by pure grace, in the Precious Blood of God's Lamb, Jesus Christ. Rom.3:24,25

The Mercy Seat was God's Throne of Grace on earth.
Heb.4:16
"Let us therefore come boldly unto the throne of grace, that we may obtain mercy, and find grace to help in time of need."

Location
The Mercy Seat was located on the Ark in the Holy of Holies.
Ex.25:21; 26:34; 40:20
It was located in the Presence of God.
2 Sam.6:2; Ps.99:1; 80:1
Where God met and manifested Himself to Moses.
Ex.25:22; Num.7:89

The Heb. word for "Mercy Seat" means
"To Atone, Covering, Propitiation" for sin.

The Mercy Seat covered Israel's sins,
speaks of the Precious Blood of Jesus covers all our sins. Jn.1:7
"If we walk in the light, as he is in the light, we have fellowship one with another, and the blood of Jesus Christ His Son cleanses us from all sin."

This covering of the Mercy Seat fitted perfectly inside the Crown of gold,
speaks of the Perfect, Complete and Immovable Atonement of the Blood of Christ.

**Purpose**
The Mercy Seat was the cover for the Ark. Ex.25:21; 26:34
It tells us of what Jesus has done for us.
Ex.25:16,21; Deut.10:2,5

The blood of bulls and goats were: sprinkled upon the Mercy Seat and before the Mercy Seat seven times. Lev.16:14,15

**Seven**, speaks of Completeness.
The Mercy Seat was the place of atonement for Israel.
The Cross of Christ is the place of atonement for us now.

On the Day of Atonement the blood of the sacrifice was sprinkled on the Mercy Seat. The Law was under the Mercy Seat. Lev.16:14,15

Man was unable to keep God's Law. The blood sprinkled upon the Mercy Seat covered God's Law. When God saw the blood upon His Law, He then descended the Holy of Holies between the Cherubim above the Mercy Seat upon the Ark in the form of His Shekinah Glory. Lev.16:2; Ex.25:22; Num.7:89

Jesus fulfilled the whole Law. Mt.5:17 He lived a perfect life, without sin. He gave Himself a perfect sacrifice to God by the shedding of His Own Blood for us.

There was made complete, once for all Atonement by the Blood of our Lord Jesus. Heb.10:10; 1 Pet.3:18; Rom.6:10

Our Lord Jesus Christ sat down on the right hand of God. Heb.4:1-11; 8:1-3; 10:11,12; 12:1,2; Rev.22:1; 3:21; Ps.110:1; Mk.16:19; Jn.19:30

Now, we may enter into the Presence of God through Him. When God looks upon us, He sees us under the Precious Blood of His Only Begotten Son!

Aaron the high priest entered into the Holy of Holies (presence of God) only once a year on the Day of Atonement.

We are in the Presence of God through the Blood of Christ by the power of His Holy Spirit.

In the earthly Tabernacle of the Exodus we see a blending of the judgment seat at the Brazen Altar and the Mercy Seat.
Ps.101:1; 85:10; 86:5,13,15; Jas.2:13

The Throne of Judgment has become a Throne of Grace.
Heb.4:14-16

Midst the Altar was a Grate. The Altar was 4 ½ ft. high. The Grate was placed 2 ft. 3 ins. from the top and 2 ft. 3 ins. from the bottom. This placed the Grate directly in the middle of the Altar. Half-way up, inside the Altar was the Grate to hold the sacrifice.

The Mercy Seat in the Holy of Holies is a type of God's throne on earth, was placed upon the Ark. The Ark was 2 ft. 3 ins. high. The Grate was on the same level as the Mercy Seat. The sacrifice was placed upon the Grate.

The supreme Sacrifice of Jesus Christ upon the Cross of Calvary was equal to the throne of God. Jesus met the claims of His Father. Death by the shedding of Blood by His Innocent Lamb to Atone for sin.

**Cherubim**, upon the mercy Seat,
speak of Jesus the Captain of our Salvation!
Heb.2:10
"It became Him (Jesus) for whom are all things, and by whom are all things, in bringing many sons unto glory, to make the Captain of their salvation perfect through suffering."

They are called:
Cherubim of Gold. Ex.25:18; 37:7
Cherubim of Glory. Heb.9:5

**Cherubim are symbols of the divine presence of God.**
Ex.25:22; Num.7:89
Examples:
God Dwells between the Cherubim.
  Ps.99:1
The Lord spoke between the Cherubim.
  Ex.25:22; Num.7:89
The Glory of God went up from the Cherubim.
  Ezek. Ch.9, v.3
The sound of their wings was as the Voice of God.
  Ezek. Ch.1, v.24; 10:5
He rode upon a Cherub, and did fly.
  Ps.18:10 etc.

**Physical Characteristics**
Ex.25:18-20; 37:7-9; Heb.9:5
Above the Mercy Seat there were two Cherubs of Gold, beaten out of one piece with the Mercy Seat. They were standing one Cherub on each end. The two Cherubim spread out their two wings on high and covered the Mercy Seat. Their wings were raised and their faces tilted down looking towards each other, They were in a praying hands, kneeling position, guarding the Mercy Seat (looking down upon the sprinkled blood upon the Mercy Seat)

## Size
No size or measurements are given for the Cherubim. They were one with the Mercy Seat. God is everywhere.
1 Kgs.8:27
"God indeed dwell on the earth? behold, the heaven and heaven of heavens cannot contain thee; "

God's mercy is great (unending)
"His mercy endures for ever ..." Ezra. 3:11

Jesus has provided the mercy of God for us through His blood sacrifice. Rom.3:24,25
The presence of God is with us now. Mt.28:20
We have eternal redemption through His blood sacrifice and will with be with God forever. Heb.9:12

## Material
The Cherubim were made of pure gold, of a beaten work.
One piece with the Mercy Seat (upon the Mercy Seat).
**Gold**, speaks of His Deity, Divinity.

## Location
Cherubim were located in three places in the Tabernacle Proper:
1. Upon the Mercy Seat in the Holy of Holies, where they are symbols of the Presence of God., speak of Jesus our way into the Presence and Kingdom of God.
2. There were Cherubim upon the Veil. Ex.26:31; 36:35
   Speak of Jesus the Guardian of our way in Holiness.
3. Cherubim were upon the Innermost Curtain in the Tabernacle Proper. Ex.26:1,31; 36:8
   Speak of Jesus, our Protector.

**Purpose**
God's Dwelling Place was here above the Ark, upon the Mercy Seat, between the two Cherubim.
Ex.25:22;
"There I will meet with thee, and I will commune with thee from between the two Cherubim which are upon the Ark of the Testimony," Num.7:89
God appeared in His Shekinah Glory.

The Mercy Seat with the Cherubim and the Ark, formed one piece of furniture.

The Ark, was covered by the priest with:
1. The Veil.
2. A badger's skin.
3. A blue cloth.
   While on the march. Num.4:5,6


When God Dwelt among the Israelites, the Ark was a symbol of His Divine Presence. It no longer exist or is necessary.
It shall never be rebuilt, because the Ark and its contents pointed to Christ.

God is not confined to one place or to one people.
God Dwells among all people, through Jesus Christ, by the power of the Holy Spirit. Jer.3:16; Jn.3:16

# Chapter 11

**The Tabernacle Proper was,
"The church in the wilderness." Ac.7:38
Tabernacle Proper, and all it's parts are a type of Christ the
Perfect Tabernacle. Heb.9:11; Col.2:9**

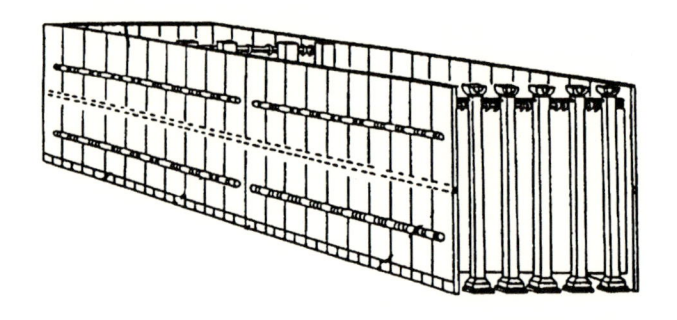

**Speaks of the great body of believers.**
Eph.2:19-22; 1 Pet.2:5

Bible study outline No.11
The believers living in the Presence of God.
In worship Doing His will and serving in His Church,
through Christ, by the power of the Holy Spirit!

Example:
**Boards**, speak of Believers.
**Silver** Sockets, speak of Redemption
**Invisible Bar**, is a type of the Holy Spirit.
**Visible Bars**, speak of the Unity of the
  Spirit in the bond of peace.
**Rings**, speak of His Unending Love.

**Physical Characteristics.** Ex.26:15-29; 36:20-34

There were 20 boards on the south and north sides. 6 boards with 2 corner boards on the west end. A total of 48 boards in all. 2 sockets under 1 board. 48 boards and 96 silver sockets for the base. Each board had 2 tenons which protruded out from the bottom end which fitted in 2 sockets. A foundation of pure silver.

The boards were supported by 5 bars of shittim wood inserted in rings of pure gold connected to the boards. One invisible bar in the center of each board that went through broadside and 4 visible outside bars.

The Tabernacle was 45 ft. long, 15 ft. wide and 15 ft. high. It was divided in 2 main parts. The Holy Place and the Holy of Holies.

The Holy Place on the east end was 30 ft. long, 15 ft. wide and 15 ft. high.

The Holy of Holies on the west end was 15 ft. long, 15 ft. wide and 15 ft. high. A perfect cube.

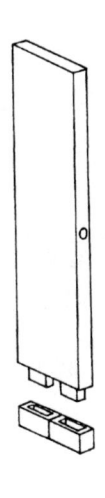

… without boards there could be no Tabernacle.
… without believers there can be no Church.

Jesus said,
"Where two or three are gathered together in my name, there am I in the midst of them. Mt 18:20
Sockets, made up the foundation of the Tabernacle, speak of Jesus, our foundation in redemption.
Jesus said,
"Upon this Rock (pointing to Himself) I will build My Church," Mt.16:18

The boards were made of shittim wood from the acacia tree.

Each board was 15 ft. high, 2 ft. 3 ins. wide.
According to the measurements of the Curtains and Coverings the boards were 9 ins. thick.

**Perfecting His Church.**
Each board represents an individual believer. If these boards could talk, "What testimony would they give to the world?

**Seven great facts of Scripture necessary to the perfecting of His Church:**

1st, before he boards could occupy a place in the Tabernacle they had to be cut down and removed from their natural standing in the world. Jn.3:3; Eph.2:1-5; Mt.3:10

We were cut down by conviction and been removed from our natural standing in the world as a person in the flesh. We now occupy our place in His Church. We have been called by God. Hos.6:5; 2 Cor.3:18; Jn.15:15-17

2$^{nd}$, the boards had to be prepared by Bezaleel. A type of the Spirit-filled believer and the wise hearted working under his direction. They were stripped, trimmed and shaped before Moses could put them into their places to form a dwelling place for God. Ac.2:47; 5:13,14

We have been born again through Christ by His Holy Spirit. The Lord added us to His Church.
1 Cor.12:13
God called us, Jesus prepared us and the Holy Spirit added us to His Church.

3$^{rd}$, each board had to be put into it's proper place by Moses (a type of Christ). Ex.40:18
The Lord called us and Jesus added us. He put us into our proper places in His Church.
Jn.4:11-24; 2 Pet.1:1-8; 1 Cor.12:13

4$^{th}$, each board rested upon two sockets of pure silver, speaks of Redemption. This was the atonement money.

We have been redeemed with the Blood of God's Perfect Lamb, our Lord and Savior, Jesus Christ. We rest in His Sacrifice. Each board stood upon two sockets of pure silver. We rest in the Sacrifice and Atonement of Christ.

5$^{th}$, each board had two tenons (hands) that protruded out from the bottom end of each board which took hold of the two sockets. A perfect fit into the sockets. They were secure. The boards with the tenons were interlocked with the silver sockets.

We hold on to His unchanging hands. We are secure in our redemption in Christ through His Blood Sacrifice. We have received the blessing in the Atonement of Christ.

6th, each board was overlaid with gold.
   **Gold**, speaks of His Deity; Divine Glory.

We have been born of the Spirit of God and are partakers of His Divine nature through the Blood of Christ. 2 Pet.1:4

The boards were of equal height,
speaks of Equality and Responsibility. They all rested on the same atonement. They were all overlaid with gold and all occupied the same nearness to God. This shows us that as to our standing before God and nearness to Him. There is no difference. We work together in fellowship and in love in His Church.

7th, each board was 1 ½ cubits (2 ft. 3 ins. wide. The half cubit,
   speaks of the Heart Revealed. God knows what is in our hearts. Heb 4:12
"The word of God is quick, and powerful, and sharper than any two edged sword, piercing even to the dividing asunder of soul and spirit, and of the joints and marrow, and is a discerner of the thoughts and intents of the heart."

We are in type the boards standing upright. Close to each other side by side in heart to heart fellowship with one another. In the Body of Christ we are beautifully set forth. We are the workmanship of God. Eph.2:10; Rom.5:5
We are the great body of believers in Christ (His Church)
He is our Testimony.

The Tabernacle rested upon the bare sand of the desert. The priests looked up at it's glorious and gorgeous golden sheeted sides and beautiful ceiling and colors.

When we consider all that the Tabernacle contains and when the Holy Spirit reveals all these things in the wonderful types of Christ there is really nothing here to satisfy our hearts.

**Wood**, overlaid with gold: Ex.26:29; 36:34
a. Wood, speaks of His Human Nature. Phil.2:7
   We have received the new birth.
   The Spiritual birth from above. Jn.3:3-7; 1:12,13
   We are born of Incorruptible Seed.1 Pet.1:23; 1 Jn.3:9
   We have His Life in us. 1 Jn.5:11,2; Col.1:27
   We are in the Father and even in the Son.
      2 Jn.9:1; 1 Jn.2:23
b. **Gold** Ex.26:29; 36:34
   Speaks of His Divine Nature. Jn.3:13; 4:42;
      10:30; Lk.1:32,35; 2:11; 20:28; 20:28;
      Ac.2:36; Rom.8:3; I Tim.6:14,15
   We are partakers of Hs Divine Nature. 2 Pet.1:4
      We live above this present evil world with all of its
      sin! Phil.4:13

**The Sockets.**
Ninety-six sockets made up the foundation of the Tabernacle Proper. These sockets weighed about 94 pounds each. Two sockets under one board making 188 pounds of pure silver under each board. The Tabernacle Proper rested upon a foundation of more than 9,000 pounds of pure silver.
b. This speaks of Jesus our Everlasting
   Foundation in Redemption. Isa.22:20-25; 28:16;
   1 Cor.3:11;Prov.10:25; 1 Pet.1:17-21.
Silver, Ex.30:11-16; 38:25-28
   The sockets were made of pure silver for the foundation
   of the Tabernacle. This was the Atonement Money.
a. Silver, speaks of His Redemption. The red coin of
   Calvary. Eph.1:7; Col.1:20; 2:14
b. We have received Eternal Redemption through the Blood
   of Christ. Heb.9:12

During the days of the Israelites slaves were bought with silver.
We have been redeemed. Purchased out of the slave market of sin through the redemptive power of the precious blood of Christ God's perfect Lamb. 1 Pet.1:18,19

Each Israelite over the age of twenty purchased his soul with ½ shekel of silver. The exact same amount of silver was required of each Israelite. The rich did not give more and the poor did not give less. Ex.30:11-16

The price for Redemption is the same for every person. Rich or poor, male or female, old or young, bond or free. All must come to God through the precious Blood of Christ for salvation. Each person must repent, confess, forsake their sins and by faith receive forgiveness through the Blood sacrifice of Christ.

Our redemption cost God the death of His Only Begotten Son by the shedding of His Blood to wash us white as snow. Isa.1:18 We are a Redeemed People.

**The Invisible inside Bar**. Ex.26:28; 36:33
   Moses caused the middle bar to shoot through each board of the Tabernacle (broadside)
a. Is a type of the Holy Spirit and a type of Christ.
b. The Holy Spirit is received through Christ.
   Jn.14:16, 26; 15:26; 16:7

He dwells in every born again believer. We are born of His Spirit. He Dwells in us and binds our hearts together in love as we look, watch and pray for each other that we enter not into temptation. Mt.26:41; Mk.14:38; Lk.21:36

**The Four Visible Bars,**
speak of Lowliness, Meekness, Longsuffering and Forbearing one another in Love.

We maintain these and the unity of the Spirit is kept in the bond of peace and the unity of His Body fully manifested.
Eph.4:2, 3

v.12
"For the perfecting of the saints, for the work of the ministry, for the edifying of the body of Christ:"

Heb.13:5
God, "Will never leave thee, nor forsake thee."

The Lord will deliver us. 2 Tim.4:18

He is able to keep us from falling. Jude 24

The **Rings**. Ex.26:29; 36:34
  Gold, on the outside bars.
a. Speak of His Unending Love for us. Jere.31:3
   God loved us. While we were yet sinners Christ died for us. Rom.5:8
b. Christ within gives us our love for Him.
   1 Jn.4:19; Jn..3:16; 1 Jn.4:9

A break down in the Tabernacle Proper and in His present day Church is impossible. All is sustained and supported by God, through Christ, by the power of the Holy Spirit.

We are His Church. We have been washed in His Precious Blood. We stand side by side and the Holy Spirit dwells in each of us and binds our hearts together with His unending love as we pray for one another that we do not enter into temptation.

The devil sees God's Church that Jesus shed His Blood and died for and he trembles.
Jas 2:19
"The devils also believe, and tremble."

We are in type and live these types. His Church is of great power. We live above this present evil world through Christ by the power of His Holy Spirit. Mt.16:18,19, 18:18-20

This is why Jesus said, "The gates of hell shall not prevail against His Church!"

**"The Word was made flesh, and dwelt
(Tabernacle) among us,
(and we beheld his glory, the glory as of the
only begotten of the Father,)
full of grace and truth."** Jn.1:14

**Tabernacle Proper with it's Inner Curtains and Outer Coverings.** Ex.26:1-14; 36:8-19

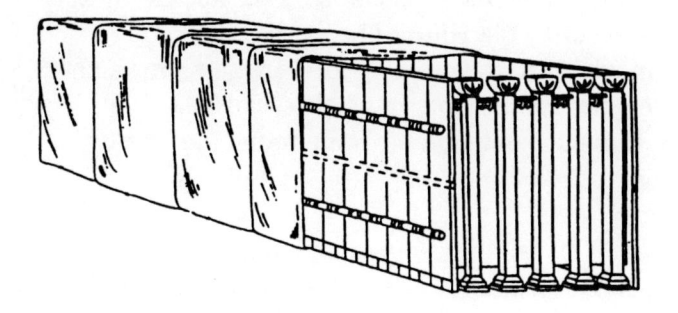

**We are a righteous, serving and devoted people to God in holiness.**

Bible study outline No.16
The Inner Curtains and Outer Coverings of the Tabernacle Proper.

1. **Fine Linen,** (of white, blue, purple and scarlet, peaks of Righteousness.
2. **Goat's hair,** (white) speaks of Service.
3. **Ram's skins,** (dyed red) speaks of Devotedness.
4. **Badger's skins,** speak of Holiness.

Eph.2:19-22

"Ye are no more strangers and foreighers, but fellow-citizens with the saints, and of the household of God; And are built upon the foundation of the apostles and prophets, Jesus Christ Himself being the chief corner stone: In whom all the building fitly framed grows unto a holy temple in the Lord: in whom we also are built together for and habitation of God through the Spirit."

1 Pet.2:5;

"Ye also as lively (living) stones, are built (be ye built) up a Spiritual house, an holy priesthood, to offer up spiritual sacrifices, acceptable to God by Jesus Christ.
Heb.8:2; Eph.3:1-21; 5:23- 33; Col.1:20-29

We are God's Spiritual House. Our bodies are the temple of the Holy Spirit. We are not our own we belong to Christ. We are bought with a price. 1 Cor.6:19,20; 3:16; Rom.14:7,8

We are the temple of the Living God. He dwells in us, He walks in us, speaks through us, He is our God and we are His people. 2 Cor.6:16; 1 Cor.3:16

The house of Christ. He is over His house  Heb.3:6

The vessels that God uses today.  2 Cor.6:14-18

The dwelling Place of God through the Holy Spirit in Jesus Christ.1 Cor.6:19,20; 2 Cor.6:14-18; 1 Cor.3:16

Believers indwelt by God through Jesus Christ by the power of the Holy Spirit. Rom.8:9-16; 1 Jn.4:13; 3:24

**The Tabernacle Proper was located in the Center of the nation of Israel. It speaks of Jesus the very heart of God.**

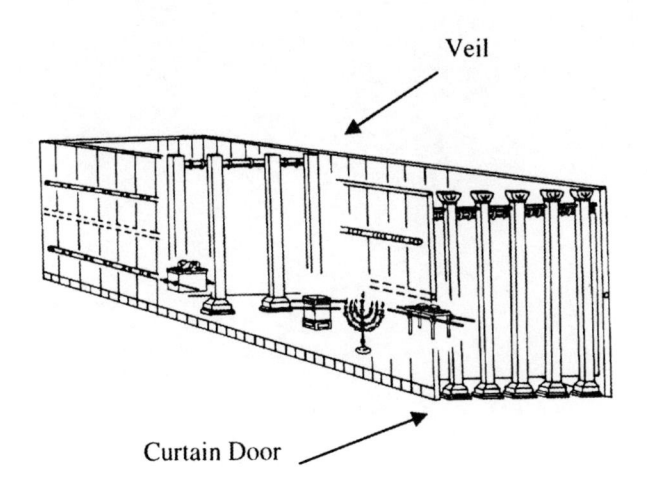

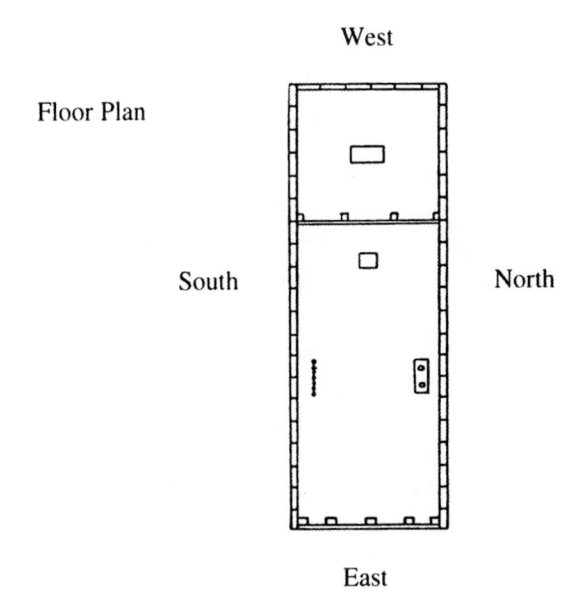

Veil

Curtain Door

West

Floor Plan

South

North

East

# Chapter 12

**The Pillar of Cloud and Fire, led the nation of Israel through the wilderness journey.**

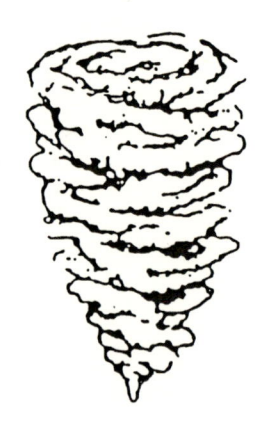

**speaks of the Holy Spirit leading us through this present evil world today.**

Bible study outline No.12
The Pillar of Cloud and Fire.
Ex.14:14,24; Num.14:14; Neh.9:12-19
1. **Visual Illustration.**
   Cloud of Glory (by day). Ex.13:21; 40:34-38
2. **Type of Christ and the Holy Spirit.**
   Rom.8:9-16; 1 Jn.4:13; 3:24
   (speaks of Christ the Anointed.
   1 Cor.10:1,2; 12:13 Ezek.43:1-5; Rev.15:5,8
   Isa.61:1-3; Lk.4:18,19; Ac.10:38; Heb.1:9; Ps.45:7)
3. **Applied to the believer.**
   Receive the Holy Spirit through Christ.
   Jn.14:16; 15:26; 16:7
4. **Believer's responsibility.**
   Follow the leading of the Holy Spirit in all things.
   Jn.16:13

1. **Visual Illustration**.
    Pillar of Fire (by night).
    Ex.13:21,22; 40:34-38
2. **Type of Christ**.
    A symbol of the Presence of God. Heb.12:29
     Jesus within us is the Presence of God!
     2 Jn.9; 1 Jn.2:23; 4:15
3. **Applied to the believer**.
    Receive the Presence of God.
    (Jesus within us is the Presence of God.
    2 Jn.9; 1 Jn.2:23; 4:15
4. **Believer's responsibility**.
    Let the Fire of God rise up in us and minister
    His Word. Ps.104:4; Heb.1:7

It was called:
- Cloud of Glory is called:
- Pillar of Cloud, and the Pillar of Fire.
    Ex.13:22; 14:19,20,24
- Cloud. Ex.16:10; 24:15,16,18; 34:5; Num.9:21
- Thick Cloud. Ex.19:9,16
- Cloudy Pillar. Ex.33:9,10
- Cloud of the Lord. Num.10:34

There was only One Pillar of both Cloud and Fire.
Ex.14:24 When the Pillar shined in the dark,
it was still called the Pillar of Cloud.
Ex.14:19
It was a Cloud Covering the Fire.

First, Israel was redeemed by the blood of the lamb and then the Cloud appeared. Ex.13:2

We were redeemed through the blood of the Lamb, Jesus Christ and then filled and led by the Holy Spirit.

The first manifestation of the Cloud is found in
Ex.13:20-22
"The Lord went before them by day in a pillar of a cloud,
 to lead them the way; and by night in a pillar of Fire, to
 give them light; to go by day and night:" v.21
The Cloud continued during the journeys of Israel.
Ex.13:22; 40:38

The Pillar of Cloud and Fire took different shapes and forms according to its purpose. When this Cloud went before the army of Israel it took the form of a column. When it stood still above or came down upon the Tabernacle it probably took the form of a round globe of cloud or a funnel. When it separated the Israelites from the Egyptians at the Red Sea, it may have spread out like a cloud bank, forming a dividing wall. Ex.14:19,20

The Pillar appeared as a Cloud in the day, in contrast with the light of the sun. A fiery splendor by night provided a celestial night light and a fiery look.
Num.9:15,16; Ps.78:14
Jesus, through the Holy Spirit is our day and night light.

They marched at all hours. God was their Divine Presence and Guidance. At night the Pillar of Fire lit up Israel's path by it's splendor. It defended Israel from terror. Ex.14:19; Ps.105:39

Protected them from their enemies.
Ps.27:1; 91:5,5
As long as they kept His commandments.
Ex.14:29, 20; 40:38; Num.9:15, 16.

The Purpose of the Cloud was for the Presence of God.
Ex.33:14,15
God's Glory was manifested in the Cloud.
Ex.16:10; 40:35

God came down in the Cloud. Ex.34:5; Num.11:25
He spoke from the Cloud. Ex.24:16; Ps.99:7

God went before them by day in a Pillar of Cloud to lead them in the way and by night in a Pillar of Fire to give Light.

God protects us from our enemies and separates us from the world as long as we obey His Spirit and keep His Word.

When God wanted to trouble the Egyptians. He looked at them with hostile gaze through the Pillar of Cloud.
Ex.14:14, 24; Num.14:14; Neh.9:12-19

The Pillar also threatened destruction to those who murmured against God. Num.17:10 and would send out Fire against the rebels and consumed them. Lev.10:2; Num.16:35

The Pillar of Cloud and Fire moved in front of the Israelites in the wilderness to show the way in which God waned them to go. Ex.13:21,22; Neh.9:19
The Holy Spirit directs our path. The way God wants us to go.

When God designed to show His Presence to the Israelite He did so in the Pillar of Cloud. Num.12:5; Deut.31:15
When God wants to show us His presence He does so in Christ through the power of the Holy Spirit.

The Cloud was a glorious light to God's people, but darkness to the enemies of Israel. Ex.14:20

Through the Cloud God manifested Himself to the nation of Israel. Deut.1:33; Num.11:25; 12:5

Through the Holy Spirit God manifests Himself to us.
Today, the Holy Spirit leads us by day and night to others for us to witness of our Lord Jesus Christ.
The Holy Spirit Lights up our path with His splendor, defends us from terror and protects us from the devil's snares and tricks. Rom.8:14; Gal.5:16-18

Jehovah's invisible Presence was with Israel. In the Cloud appeared "the Glory of the Lord" and He spoke to them out of the Cloud. Ex.16:10; 40:34; Num.17:7
The Lord speaks to us by the Holy Spirit through His Word and His Glory is seen in and through Jesus Christ.

As long as the Pillar of Cloud and Fire was with Israel they knew the Lord was in their midst. The Pillar of Cloud never left them. It remained with them until they were brought into the land. The Holy Spirit will remain with us until we enter heaven and throughout all eternity.

The Pillar of Cloud and Fire was located above, within the Tabernacle and on the march day and night. The Fire in the Pillar was the same as that in which the Lord revealed Himself to Moses in the burning bush. Ex.3:2,3
The same Fire that afterward descended upon Mt. Sinai amid thunder and lightning. Ex.19:16-18

The same Fire (Shekinah Glory) that descended upon the Mercy Seat between the two cherubim above the Ark in the Holy of Holies on the Day of Atonement.

The Cloud Manifested in the Temple of Solomon.
1 Kgs.8:10,11; 2 Chron.5:13; Ezek.10:4

The Cloud (of Glory) was Present At Christ's Transfiguration. Mt.17:5
The Voice of God comes from a Cloud. Mk.9:7
At Christ's Ascension. Ac.1:9

Jesus is received up in a Cloud into Heaven.
Ac.1:9; 1 Kgs.8:10,11
Our Lord shall make His Second Appearance in the Cloud. Lk.21:27; Ac.1:11

The Cloud is a symbol of the Divine Presence of God and a type of the Holy Spirit with us now, today in Christ.

---

In the Gospel of John, chs.14-16 is recorded Seven Things the Holy Spirit (Comforter) will do when He comes:
1. "He shall **Teach** you all things," 14:26
2. "Bring All Things to your **Remembrance**," 14:26
3. "He shall **Testify** of Me (Jesus):" 15:26
4. "He will **Reprove** (convict) the world of sin," 16:8
5. "He will **Guide** you into all Truth:" 16:13
6. "Will **Shew** you Things to Come." 16:13
7. "He will **Glorify** Me (Jesus):" 16:14

The Cloud of Glory is the Holy Spirit within. He gives us salvation. The Pillar of Fire is the Holy Spirit upon gives us power to witness.

# Chapter 13

## The Day of Atonement

**DAY OF ATONEMENT**
Heb. Yom Kippur Tishri
7$^{th}$ month, 10$^{th}$ day Sept.– Oct.
**High priest in his pure white holy linen garments, worn only on the Day of Atonement in the Holy of Holies within the Veil. Lev.16:4**

**After DeVries JHK**

**Shekinah Glory**. Lev.16:2
"The Lord said, to Moses, Speak to Aaron your brother, that he come not at all times into the holy place (Holy of Holies) within the veil before the mercy seat which is upon the ark: that he die not:for I will appear in the cloud (**Shekinah Glory**) upon the mercy seat. Ex.25:22; Num.7:89

The Day of Atonement is described in
Lev.16:3, 5-11 here are detailed instructions for the high priest's duties concerning the sin offerings.
ch.23:26-32 describes holy convocation when Israel afflicted their souls by fasting.
Num.29:7-11 gives information concerning the other offerings offered on this most holy day.

**Preparation**
All of the tasks preformed on the Day of Atonement had to be carried out by the high priest himself.

**Four Sacrifices Offered on the Day of Atonement from Lev.16:3,5-11**
v.3, First, "**A young bullock** for a sin offering,"
The bullock was killed for a sin offering at the Brazen Altar to make an atonement for Aaron and his household. v.6,11
(Heb.5:2,3; 7:27,28) 9:7-8:2
Aaron and his sons laid their hands upon the head of the sacrifice. Ex.12:27; 29:10
They confessed their sins and transferred them to the bullock. Atonement for sin was made. Ex.29:10-14; Lev.8:14-17; Heb.9:26; 11:4
The blood was put upon the horns of the Brazen Altar and this purified it. The blood of the sin offering alone was poured at the bottom of the Altar.Ex.29:12; Lev.4:7,18,25,30,34; 9:9; 5:9

This altar with it's sacrifice,
speaks of God's Holy Lamb, Jesus Christ without sin or blemish.
I Pet.1:19
Our Great High Priest Jesus offered Himself in Sacrifice by shedding His Own Precious Blood for our sins on the Cross of Calvary.
2 Cor.5:21; Heb.9:26; 10:12 ; 1 Pet.2:24; Heb.4:15; 1 Pet.2:22; Heb.7:26; 1 Jn.3:5

v.3 Next, "**A ram** for a burnt offering." v.24;
Ex.29:15-18; Lev.8:18-21
The highest sacrifice in Scripture. All of it's fragrance and odor ascends from off the Fire of the Brazen Altar as a sweet savor to the Lord. Burnt Offering, that which "ascends" or "goes up."

Eph.5:2 Jesus has,
"Given Himself for us an offering and a sacrifice to God
 for a sweet smelling savor."
Jesus was called to holiness. He lived His life unto His Father.

We are called to holiness. 1 Thes.4:7; 2 Pet.1:4
"What kind of an odor are we sending up to God?"
Heb.13:15 through Christ,
"Let us offer the sacrifice of praise to God continually, that is,
 the fruit of our lips giving thanks to His Name."

"He offered the sacrifice of his own voluntary
 will." Lev.1:3

Jesus offered Himself of His own voluntary will.
Jn.10:18, Jesus said,
 "No man takes My life from Me, but I lay it down of Myself.
 I have power to lay it down, and I have power totake it again."

Nearly 600 years before it came to pass Isaiah the prophet of Redemption said, Jesus will be, "Brought as a Lamb to the slaughter," Isa.53:7

Luke said, Jesus "Was led as a Sheep to the slaughter;" Ac.8:32

We reach the highest standing in God by doing what God tells us to do willingly.

Example:
"Present your bodies a living sacrifice, holy acceptable unto
  God, which is your reasonable service." Rom.12:1

Jesus went willingly to be Sacrificed. It cost Jesus everything when He walked up the hill to Calvary to redeem us.
The redeemed are willing to serve Him out of gratitude!
Jn.12:26; Rom.1:9; Gal.5:13; Col.3:24

v.5,7-10, Third, "**two goats** for a sin offering."
He casts lots upon the two goats: one lot for the Lord, a sin offering for the people. v.15,
Speaks of the death of Jesus Christ.
The other lot for the scapegoat for atonement.
These two goats were one sin offering.
Isa.1:18 tells us to,
"Come now, and let us reason together, saith the Lord:
  though your sins be as scarlet, they shall be as white as
  snow; though they be red like crimson, they shall be as wool."

A type of Christ the Faithful Witness!
Rev.1:5
"Unto Jesus that loved us, and washed us from
  our sins in His Own Blood." 1 Pet.1:19; Rev.5:9

v.5 , And, "**One ram** for a burnt offering." v.24;
Ex.29:19,20; Lev.8:22-24
"The ram of consecration;"
Ex.29:22,26,27,34; Lev.9:22,29

Aaron and his sons laid their hands upon the head of this ram. It was killed. The blood was put on the tip of their right ear, thumb of the right hand and the great toe of the right foot.
29:20; Lev.8:23,24

The blood of Christ applied by faith, spiritually to our ears, represents **Consecrated Hearing**.
Mt.7:24; 13:15; 16:43; Zech.7:11
We listen to the voice of God.

The blood of Christ applied by faith, spiritually to our thumbs, represents **Consecrated Service**.
1 Tim.2:8; 5:22; Eph.4:28
Hands, speak of Service. We service to God.

The blood of Christ applied by faith spiritually to our toes, (feet) represent **Consecrated Walk**.
1 Jn.1:7; 2:6
Feet, speak of our walk in God.

We walk in God. We live a consecrated,
separated life unto God. A living example of Christ,
by the power of the Holy Spirit.

Aaron's sons the ministering priests,
speak of us the believers. Through Jesus Christ we are the priesthood of believers. We have been called, saved and dedicated to God through the blood of Christ. We are called to salvation and called to holiness. Mt.9:13; 1 Thess.4:3-7

All the priests were dedicated to God by blood,
speaks of separation from the world.

**v.4, Aaron bathed his flesh in water.**
He took a bath with the water he took from the lower part of the Laver.
Water, speaks of the Cleansing and Sanctification.
Jesus sanctifies and cleanses us with the washing of water by His Word. Eph.5:26

**The Holy Linen Garments.**
After the high priest took a bath from the Laver he put on the pure white Holy Linen Garments.
He put on the
1. **Coat**, speaks of the Righteousness and Spotless Purity of Christ.
2. **Breeches**, speaks of the Perfect Provision God has made for us in Christ.
   **Girdle**, speaks of His Perfect Service.
3. **Mitre**, speaks of the Authority of Jesus Christ.

The high priest wore all spotless pure white holy linen garments from head to foot on the Day of Atonement. v.32

**They speak of the Personal Righteousness and Holiness of our Lord and Savior, Jesus Christ the Perfect One.**
Heb.7:26
"For such and High Priest (Jesus) became us, who is holy, harmless, undefiled, separate from sinners, and made higher than the heavens;"

**Spotless White Linen,** speaks of the Holy Humanity of Christ.

End of preparation

---

**THE DAY OF ATONEMENT** was a fast day on which no work was done. It was observed in the seventh month. On the tenth day of the month. Lev.16:29; 23:22 -31; Num.29:7
Aaron the high priest took Live Coals of Fire from off the Brazen Altar in the Outer Court. He put them in a Golden Censer, beforehand and placed them upon the Golden Altar to burn incense in the Holy Place . He then took the Golden Censer with the Live Coals of Fire from the Golden Altar to burn incense when needed.
The Golden Altar to burn incense speaks of Jesus our Intercessor. Rom.8:34; Heb.7:25 tells us that,
Jesus is at the right hand of the Father. He ever lives to make Intercession for us.

Aaron went into the Holy Place where he took up the Golden Censer which was full of burning coals of Fire from upon the Golden Altar to burn incense. He also picked up sweet incense, and brought it within the Veil into the Holy of Holies.

**Sweet Incense**, speaks of Jesus our sweet smelling savor. Lev.1:9 Eph.5:2
"Walk in love, as Christ also hath loved us, and hath given Him self for us an offering and a sacrifice to God for a sweet smelling savor." 2 Cor.2:25

v.13 Aaron put the incense upon the Fire before the Lord. The cloud of the incense covered and screened the Mercy Seat that is upon the testimony, that he die not: Lev.6:13
(Aaron's first entrance into the Holy of Holies within the Veil).

When Aaron put the incense upon the Live Coals of Fire, it caused a cloud of smoke to billow up and cover the Mercy Seat. The cloud of Incense was between the high priest and the Shekinah Glory upon the Mercy Seat above the Ark. The Presence of God appeared behind the cloud of Incense. The smoke shielded him from the Shekinah Glory, so that he die not.

Lev.16:14
Aaron took of the blood of the bullock and sprinkled it with his finger upon the mercy seat eastward; and before the mercy seat seven times."
(His second entrance into the Holy of Holies, within the Veil).

Aaron took the blood from his own sin offering and sprinkled it upon the Mercy Seat and before the Mercy Seat seven times.

He had bathed his flesh, put on the holy linen garments and is now sheltered under a cloud of incense. He was covered by the blood of the sin offering.

The blood of the sin offering was sprinkled through the cloud of incense.
(He backed out of the Holy of Holies into the Holy Place).

When Aaron entered through the veil it was completely dark. The first Light in the Holy of Holies on the Day of Atonement was the Light from the glowing Live Coals of Fire in the Golden Censor.

This Fire came from the Shekinah Glory from off the Golden Altar to burn incense which was taken from the Brazen Altar where God Lit His Fire.

The Golden Censer was the vessel that held the Fire.
The Live Coals of Fire,
are a type of the Holiness of God.
Speaks of Jesus the Holiness of God. The golden censer was full. Jesus is full. The Holy One of Israel is mighty in Holiness.
Ac.13:35
"Without holiness no man shall see God." Heb.12:14

v.9,15
Aaron Sprinkled the blood of the goat upon the Mercy Seat. the sin offering for the people, between the staves. He sprinkled the blood of the goat with his finger upon the Mercy Seat and before the Mercy Seat seven times Eastward.
(His third entrance into the Holy of Holies, within the Veil).

The first goat, the Lord's for the people was offered on the Brazen Altar for a sin offering, because without the shedding of blood there could be no remission of sin.
Lev.17:11
"The life of the flesh is in the blood: I have given it to you upon the altar to make an atonement for your souls: it is the blood that makes an atonement for the soul."

A type of Christ's death upon the Cross of Calvary.
Heb.9:22 "Without shedding of blood is no remission."

Mt.26:28 Jesus said,
"This is My Blood of the new testament, which is
  shed for many for the remission of sins."

The Mercy Seat above the Ark was the Throne of Glory where God manifested His Presence, between the two Cherubim in the form of His Shekinah Glory.

---

**Once a year on the Day of Atonement** the high priest entered through the Veil into the Holy of Holies with the blood of the sin offering. He made an atonement for the sins of the nation of Israel. He sprinkled the blood upon and before the Mercy Seat, Eastward seven times.
When the blood of the sin offering was sprinkled upon the Mercy Seat God saw the blood upon His Law which was beneath the Mercy Seat in the Ark. When God saw the blood then He Descended the Holy of Holies and Appeared upon the Mercy Seat between the two Cherubim which were above the Ark of the Testimony in the form of His **Shekinah Glory**.
Ex.25:22; Num.7:89; 20:6; Lev.9:23,24

This is a type of Christ. Jesus fulfilled the Whole Law. Mt.5:17 Not just the Ten Commandments, but 613 commandments and 213 health laws.
Our sins have been forgiven. We have been washed, sprinkled and covered: When God looks upon our hearts He sees us under the Precious Blood of Christ. Rev.1:5,6

**Jesus is the Shekinah Glory.**
Jn.17:5
"He prayed, "Father, glorify Thou Me with Thine Own Self
  with the glory which I had with Thee before the world was."
  v.24; Jn.1:1,14

Rev.21:23
"The City had no need of the sun, neither of the moon, to shine in it: for the Glory of God did Lighten it, and the Lamb (Jesus Christ) is the Light thereof."
The Father and His Son are the light of the Holy City, the New Jerusalem.

"Jesus is the brightness of God's glory, and the express image of God's Person," Heb.1:3

The Presence of God dwells within us through Christ now by the power of the Holy Spirit.
Rom.8:9-16; 1 Jn.4:13; 3:24 ; Ps.104:4; Heb1:7
(He backed out of the Holy of Holies, from within the veil.

**Aaron made an Atonement for the** Holy of Holies, Holy Place, himself, household and the Congregation of Israel, because of their sin. v.16

The Holy Place is a type of the Church. Ps.93:5
**"Holiness becometh Thine house, O Lord, for ever."**

Jesus said,
"My house shall be called the house of prayer by all nations."
Mk.11:17

v.17
"There was no man in the Holy Place when Aaron went in to make an atonement in the Holy of Holies, until he came out, and made an atonement for himself, his household and for all the congregation of Israel."

No one was with the high priest or entered the Tabernacle until he had completed that important work of atonement. It was accomplished by the high priest alone.

Jesus, our Great High Priest made an Atonement for our soul by the shedding of His Own Blood. Our Atonement was accomplished by Him alone.

**While Aaron was still in the Tabernacle he made an Atonement for the altar that is before the Lord.**
He went out to the altar (to burn incense) that was before the Lord and make an atonement for it and took of the blood of the bullock and of the goat. He put it upon the horns of the altar to burn incense round about." Altar, only for God.
v.18; Ex.30:8-10; Lev.4:3-7,18

The rest of the blood was sprinkled on it with His finger seven times cleanse and hallow it from the uncleanness of the children of Israel." v.19

"The Altar before the Lord" mentioned here is the Golden Altar to burn incense located in the Holy Place . The expression, "Altar before the Lord" refers only to the Altar to burn Incense in the Holy Place.

The Brazen Altar in the Outer Court (a holy altar) is never referred to as being "Before the Lord."
The blood of the bullock, (sin offering for Aaron and his house) and the blood of the goat, (sin offering for the people,) was put upon the horns of the Golden Altar to burn incense, and sprinkled seven times upon this Altar , as the blood of the same sin offering had been sprinkled before on the Mercy Seat and Ark. This cleansed and hollowed the Golden Altar to burn incense from the uncleanness of the children of Israel. Ex.30:10

Aaron did not go out of the Tabernacle Proper itself into the Outer Court until after he had finished the work of atonement towards God, for himself, the people and also had cleansed the Holy Places. He only went out of the Holy of Holies where the

Ark of the Covenant stood, through the veil back out into the Holy Place where the Golden Altar to burn incense, the Table of Shewbread and the Candlestick stood.
(The Altar to burn Incense was always located in the Holy Place) Ex.30:6-8; 40:22,24,26

v.20 "When he hath made an end of reconciling the Holy of Holies, and the Holy Place, and the Altar to burn incense he shall bring the live goat:

**Aaron let go the scapegoat into the wilderness.**
The high priest went out of the Holy Place into the Outer Court. Lev.16:21
"Aaron laid both his hands upon the head of the live goat. He confess over him all the iniquities of the children of Israel and all their transgressions in all their sins. He put them upon the head of the live goat. He let go the scapegoat, unto a land not inhabited. Sent him away by the hand of a fit man into the wilderness." Lev.16:5,7-10,26
v.22
The live goat was taken far out, away from the Tabernacle and let go so that it could not find his way back. Their sin was taken away, out of the camp. Ps.103:12; Isa.53:11,12; Jn.1:29

All the sins, iniquities, transgressions, trespasses, evils, errors, secret faults, presumptuous sins and wickedness.

The only sin that was not taken away was the sin committed against a neighbor.
Jesus said,
"If we sin against our neighbor, we must go to that person and ask forgiveness." Mt.5: 22:26 ; 18:15:20

Jesus is our Scapegoat. He has taken away all our sins. He made one sacrifice for sin for all time.
Heb.9:28
"So Christ was once offered to bear the sins of many;"
  Rom.6:10; Heb.7:27; 9:12 ,28; 10:10; 1 Pet.3:18
Jesus has taken away all our sins with His Own Blood.
Heb.10:17
"Their sins and iniquities will I remember no more."

The purpose for the second goat which was the scapegoat for atonement, speaks of Jesus. He has taken away all our sins.

v.23 "Aaron came into the Holy Place, and put off the pure white holy linen garments, which the put on when he went into the Holy of Holies, and left them there:" (in a chamber)

v.24 "He washed his flesh with water in the Holy Place and put on his garments."

**He put on the seven piece garments of glory and beauty.**

In addition to the coat, breeches with the girdle and the mitre, he put on the colored garments of glory and beauty:

4. **Robe**, of the ephod, speaks of The Divinity of Christ.
   Pomegranates, speak of Fruitfulness.
   Bells, speak of Testimony and Praise.
5. **Ephod**, speaks of the Position, Office and Character of Christ.
6. **Breastplate, of Judgment,**
    speaks of Jesus the Loving One.
       Stones, are a type of believers.
       Breast, speaks of Affection.
       Heart, is the symbol of Love.
       Urim and Thummim, in the pouch.
       speak of Jesus Christ the Light, Perfection, Illumination and Truth.

7.. **Curious Girdle,**
    speaks of A Gathering (binding) Together.
    Golden Plate, with the inscription upon it,
    "HOLINESS UNTOTHE LORD."
    Head, is a symbol of the Mind.
A Blue Lace, under the Plate, speaks of
Jesus the Heavenly Minded One.
All of these colored garments, speak of the believers in a secondary type.
Seven articles of clothing, speak of Divine Perfection.

High Priest in his seven-piece garments of glory and beauty.
        Ex.28:1-43; 29:1-28; 39:1-31
A type of Christ our Great High Priest High and Exalted.
        Heb.7:24-26; 8:1,2

Aaron did not ware his seven-piece garments of glory and beauty in the Holy of Holies.

**PASSOVER** (Unleaven Bread)
Nisan (Abib) 14-21 March – April

At Calvary Jesus the Innocent One died for the guilty.
Mt.27:50; Mk.15:37; Lk.23:46; Isa.53:12

When Jesus died upon the Cross of Calvary for our sins.
Isa.53:11,12; 1 Pet.2:24

God rent the Veil (tore in two pieces) from top to bottom.
Mt.27:51; Mk.15:38 Lk.23:45;Jn.2:19-22

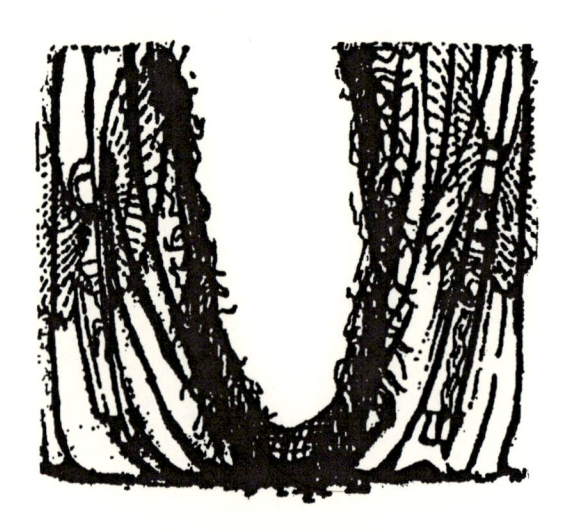

This is the only act in the entire Bible where God represents Himself. When He rent the Veil and smote His Only Begotten Son, the Lord Jesus Christ.
Mt.26:31; Mk.14:27; Isa.53:4; Zech.13:7

This ended the earthly priesthood. We no longer need a high priest to represent us before God and to make an atonement for our souls, because Jesus, "Offered one sacrifice for sins for ever," Heb.10:12; 7:26, 27; 9:12-14, 23-26; Rom.6:10

We may enter now into the Presence of God through the Precious Blood of Christ!
Heb.10:19,20
"Having therefore, brethren, boldness to enter into the holiest by the blood of Christ.
By a new and living way, which He hath consecrated for us, through the veil, that is to say, His Flesh;" 6:19,20
Jesus is our **one and only** Great High Priest. We have Him to represent us before God. Heb.7:26; 4:14 ; 1 Tim.2:5

... can you imagine the high priest going about his daily service in the Holy Place , arranging the bread on the Table, burning the sweet incense and dressing the Lamps.
The golden bells on the hem of his robe sent up a glorious sound that he was about His Father's
service.

--- and then suddenly, God, Himself rent the Veil in two!
This took place in the temple. Jn.2:20-22; Mt.27:51,52

Jn.3:16
"For God so loved the world, that He gave His only begotten Son, that whosoever believeth in Him should not perish, but have everlasting life." Rom.5:8; 1 Jn.4:9

God sent His Only Begotten Son to redeem a lost world. When Jesus died upon the Cross of Calvary for our sins, He became sin for us.
2 Cor.5:21
"He hath made Him (Jesus) to be sin for us, who knew no sin; that we might be made the righteousness of God in Him." Isa.6,11

When Jesus was made sin for us, God lifted His Presence. Turned His back on His Only Begotten Son temporarily, because God can not be contaminated with sin. He can not look at sin with approval, nor can He allow it.

God turned His back on His Only Begotten Son. This is how much God hates sin. This by far is worse than the tremendous suffering Jesus received to redeem us.

When God looked away from Jesus, the sun was darkened, the earth did quake and the rocks rent. Mt.27:51; Lk.23:45

Jesus said,
"My God, My God, why hast Thou forsaken Me? Mt.27:46; Mk.15:34; Ps.22:1

After the Atonement was made the cleansing Blood of Jesus purged away our sin that was laid upon Him (our sin Jesus had no sin). God then restored His Presence on to Christ.

Jesus said, He would be crucified and rise again the third day.
Mt.16:21; Mk.8:31; 9:31 ; Lk.9:22; 24:7

Jesus Resurrected from the dead, as He said He would. He burst the bands of death, victor over sin, hell and death.
Mt.28:6,7; Mk.16:6,7; Lk.24:6-9; Jn.20:6-9

In the New Testament when the death of Jesus is mentioned the fact of His Resurrection always follows. These two teachings are always mentioned together.

Example:
1 Cor.15:3-4
"I delivered unto you first of all that which I also received, how that Christ died for our sins according to the scriptures;
And that He was buried, and that He rose again the third day according to the scripture:"

**Appearances of Jesus Christ after His resurrected, before He ascended into heaven:**
1. He showed Himself alive to Mary Magdalene weeping at His tomb. Jn.20:14; Mk.16:9
2. To the other women. Mt.2
3. To Peter. 1 Cor.15:5; Lk.24:34
4. To the two disciples on their way to Emmaus. Mk.16:12,13; Lk.24:13-32
5. The day He appeared to the disciples, in the absence of Thomas. Jn.20:19-24
6. To the disciples when Thomas was present. Jn.20:24-29
7. In Galilee, at the sea of Tiberias, to Peter, John, Thomas, James, Nathaneal, and two others. Jn.21:1-14
8. To more than five hundred brethren at once.1 Cor.15:6
9. To James the people. 1 Cor.15:7
10. To all the apostles assembled together.1 Cor.15:7
11. To all the apostles at His Ascension.Lk.24:50,51
12. After Jesus ascended into heaven He appeared to Stephen. Ac.7:56
13. To Paul at his conversion on the road to Damascus. 1 Cor.15:8; Ac.9:3-5; 22:6-10; 23:11
14. To John on the isle of Patmos. Rev.1:12-18

Jesus appears to all who repent of their sins and ask Him into their heart.
v.17
"If Christ be not raised, our faith is vain; we are yet in sins."
v.20
"But now is Christ risen from the dead, and become the First Fruits of them that slept."

If we do not believe that Jesus Rose from the dead, we can not be saved. Rom.10:9

**Jesus prophesied of His own death and Resurrection**:
Mt.16:21; 17:23; 20:19; Mt.27:63-66

**The apostles preached Christ's Resurrection from the dead**
(eyewitnesses). Ac.2:24,29-33; 3:15,26; 4:10:33; 5:30;
9:5; 10:40,41; 13:30-34,37; 17:3,18,31; 26:23; Rom.1:4;
4:24,25; 6:4,9; 7:4; 8:11,34

Rom.10:9; 1 Cor.6:14; 15:4,12-15,20; 2 Cor.4:14;
5:15; Gal.1:1; Eph.1:20; Phil.3:10; Col.2:12; 3:1;
1 Thess.1:10; 4:14; 2 Tim.2:8; Heb13:20; 1 Pet.1:3; 3:21;
Rev.1:18; 2:8; 5:5-8; 22:7,12,16,20

After He Resurrected, Jesus prophesied to Mary,
"Touch Me not; for I am not yet ascended to My Father."
Jn.20:17
He said this because He had not yet taken His Atoning
Blood to His Father in Heaven. Heb.9:14

When Jesus came back to earth and showed Himself alive for
forty days, all of His disciples touched and worshiped Him.
Mt.28:9; Ac.1:1-4

Jesus, "Was received up into heaven, and sat on the right hand of God." Ac.1:9; Mk.16:19; Lk.24:51; Jn.20:17; Eph.4:8; Ac.1:2

-through His death, we receive forgiveness from sin.
-through His resurrection, we receive everlasting life.
-through His ascension, we receive His power to live above this present evil world, because He sent us His Holy Spirit!

**Garments for Aaron's son the priest.**
Ex.28:40; 29:8,9; 39:27,28; Lev.8:13

They were arrayed in pure white garments
of fine linen:
1. **Coats**, speak of Salvation. Isa.61:10
2. **Girdles**, speak of Service. Ps.100:2
3. **Breeches**, speak of Self-effacement (humility) Submission, obedience.Gal.3:1-3; 5:7; 1 Pet.1:22,23
   We are the priesthood of believers.
   Ex.19:5; 1 Pet.2:7-9; Rev.1:6; 5:10 ; 20:6
4. **Bonnets**, speak of Subjection. Heb.12:9
   These are the garments of Aaron's sons the priest.

Only the priest could enter the Tabernacle. Num.18:3,5 They performed all the services. Num.3:10; 18:1,2; Heb.9:6 They were the ministers of the Tabernacle. Heb.8:2

These priests had no access into the Holy of Holies. Aaron is a type of the only high priest we have which is the Lord Jesus Christ.

Jesus is the Father's salvation for the whole world.
 1 Jn.2:2 Jesus,
"Is the propitiation for our sins: and not for ours
  only, but also for the sins of the whole world."

Our message is: the Veil was rent by God Himself when Jesus died upon the Cross of Calvary by the shedding of His Own Precious Blood for our sins. We may now enter into the Presence of God through the Blood of Christ.

Heb.10:19, 20
"Having therefore, brethren, boldness to enter into
  the holiest by the **blood of Christ**.
  By a new and living way, which He hath cones
  crated for us, through the veil, that is to say, **His Flesh**;"
  6:19, 20; 9:12

**Jesus is:**
**The Lamb of God.** Jn.1:29, 36
**Our Great High Priest.** Heb.7:26
**The Good Shepherd.** Jn.10:11, 14
**Prophet – Priest – King!**

All who have received forgiveness from sin through the Blood of Christ is a type of Aaron's sons, the priests.
Through Jesus Christ we are the priesthood of believers.
A royal priesthood.
A kingdom of priests.
Ex.19:5; 1 Pet.2:7-9; Rev.1:6; 5:10; 20:6

**Where are you located in the "Circle of Faith?**
Are you:
Standing way off in the distance. Far away from Christ like the 500 brethren. 1 Cor.1:15:6
"Jesus was seen of above five hundred brethren at once; of whom the greater part remain unto this present, but some are fallen asleep (have died)."
One of the 70 that Jesus would send where He Himself would go. Lk.10:1
"After these things the Lord appointed other seventy also, and sent them two and two before his face into every city and place, whither He Himself would come."
One of the 12 disciples that dwelt with Him always and was within His private ministry and went where He went and did what He did. Mt.10:1; Mk.3:16; Lk.6:14; Ac.1:13
One of the 3 in the Mount Transfiguration. Seeing His Glorious Resurrection Body. Mt.17:2
Jesus, "was transfigured before them: and his face did shine as the sun, and his raiment was white as the light."
(This was not His full glory which Jesus had with His Father before the world was. This was only a measure of His glorious, magnificent resurrection body. See Rev.1:12-20).
One who laid his head upon the breast of Jesus. Jn.13:23,25
"Now there was leaning on Jesus' bosom one of His disciples, whom Jesus loved."

Heb 10:19,20
"Having therefore, brethren, boldness to enter into the holiest by the **blood of Jesus**, By a new and living way, which he hath consecrated for us, through the veil, that is to say, **His flesh**;

---

**Tabernacle in Heaven**:
   Rev.21:2,3; 13:6; 15:5; Heb.9:23,24; 8:5
**Shekinah Glory**. Rev.1:16; 23:33-25
**Cloud of Glory**. Rev.15:5,8; Ezek.43:1-5
**Seraphim**. Isa.6:1-8  (Rev.4:1-11 by implication).
**Cherubim**. Ezek.1:5; 10:20* Chs.1,2
**Mercy Seat**. (God's Throne in Heaven) Rev.3:21; 4:2,3
**Ark** (of His Testimony). Rev.11:19
   a. **Law**. Rev.11:19
   b. **Manna** (hidden) Rev.2:17
**Veil Rent**. Rev.11:19; 15:5
   The Veil in Heaven is Now Open through the Blood of Jesus, because He made an Atonement for our souls. Rev.11:19; 15:5; Heb.10:12
**Table of Shewbread.** (See Golden Altar).
Golden Altar (to burn incense) Rev.8:3
   a. **Golden Censer**. Rev.8:3
   b. **Incense**. Rev.8:3
**Golden Candlestick**. Rev.1:12,13
**Laver**. Rev.4:6; 15:2
Brazen Altar (of burnt-offering)
Lamb. Jesus. Rev.5:6,8; 7:17
**Blood**, of Jesus. Rev.1:5,6; 5:9

Only the precious, innocent blood of our Lord and Savior Jesus Christ the Only Begotten Son of God is in heaven!

**Shekinah**, is a Heb. Word from the root **"To Dwell."** It is translated the **"Presence of God."**
The **Shekinah Glory** that appeared upon the Mercy Seat is a reality. A Manifestation.
The **Actual, Visible Presence of Jehovah**.
The **Shekinah Glory** is not a reality separate from God.
Examples:
The priestly word for the **tent of meeting**, comes from the same root as **Shekinah**.
The Glory of God which filled the Tabernacle with **His Shekinah**.
**God's Shekinah** is referred to in:
Ex.25:22; 29:42, 43, 45; Lev.9:23, 24; 16:2; Num.7:89; 20:6
"**Shekinah**" Isa.60:2  "**His Glory**" Rom.9:4
"**The Glory**" Ex.14:19, 20  "**The Cloud**" Ex.13:21
"**Pillar of Cloud and Fire**" etc.

God often veils Himself in a Cloud.
Ex.24:15-18; 34:5; 40:34-38  (1 Kgs.8:10, 11- 2 Chron.5:13, 14)

## THE SHEKINAH GLORY "CLOUD OF GOD."
1. Led Israel across the wilderness.
    Ex.13:21-22; Num.9:17-22
2. Protected Israel at the Red Sea. Ex.14:19-20, 24
3. Appeared when Israel murmured in the Zin wilderness.
    Ex.16:10
4. Appeared when God spoke to Moses on Mount Sinai.
    Ex.19:9, 16; 24:15-16, 18; 34:5
5. Filled the Tabernacle during Moses' dedication. Ex.40:34-38
6. Stood above the mercy seat in the Holy of Holies. Num.16:2
7. Appeared when God appointed the 70. Num.11:25
8. Appeared when Miriam spoke against Moses' wife.12:5
9. Appeared as Moses pleaded for Israel. Num.14:14
10. Appeared during Korah's rebellion. Num.16:42
11. Filled the temple during Solomon's dedication.
    1 Kgs.8:10-11; 2 Chron.5:13,14
12. Was seen by Ezekiel. Ezek.1:28; 8:11; 10:3-4
13. Appeared to the shepherds at Christ's birth. Lk.2:8-9
14. Was present at Christ's baptism. Mt.3:16
15. Was present at Christ's transfiguration. Mt.17:5
16. Was present at Christ's death. Mt.27:45
17. Was present at Christ's ascension. Ac.1:9
18. Will appear at the Rapture.1 Thess.4:17
19. Will appear during the Tribulation at the funeral of God's two witnesses. Rev.11:12
20. Will appear during the Second Coming.
    Dan.7:13-14; Mt.24:30; Rev.1:7; 14:14

# Chapter 14

Jesus sacrificed past, Presence and future.

a. In Rev.13:8 The Lamb Slain,
   "From the foundation of the world."
b. In Ex. Ch.12 The Passover lamb slain in Egypt.
   1 Cor.5:7
   speaks of "Christ our Passover is Sacrificed for us:"
c. In Ex.29:38-41 The Lamb slain in the Tabernacle Courtyard upon the Brazen Altar for the sacrifice of sin by the shedding of blood is a type of God's Perfect Lamb, Jesus Christ our Redeemer.
   Jn.1:29
   "Behold the Lamb of God, which takes away the sin of the world." v.36
   1 Pet.1:19 We were Redeemed,
   "With the Precious Blood of Christ, as of a Lamb without blemish and without spot:
d. In Isa.53:7,11; Ac. 8:32
   The Lamb slain in prophecy. Jesus,
   "Is brought as a Lamb to the slaughter."
e. In Mt.27:35 The Lamb of God actually Slain. Jesus took the form of flesh, lived a Perfect Life, gave Himself a Sacrifice for our sins, by shedding His Own Blood on the Cross (Altar) of Calvary. Mk.15:24 "They Crucified Jesus," Lk.23:33; Jn.19;23.
f. In Rev.5:6 The Lamb of God in Heaven .Jesus is standing as, "A Lamb as it had been slain," Rev.7:17 Jesus is, "In the midst of the Throne ."

## JESUS IS THE PERFECT LAMB OF GOD!

The Passover. Ex.12:1-36
Speaks of Israel's deliverance from captivity and death
Ex. 12:3-5,11-13
The angel of death passed over and killed the firstborn son of every home in Egypt. The firstborn sons of the Israelites were spared. They did not die because a lamb had been slain and the blood was placed on the two side posts and over the door of every house. God said,
"When I see the blood, I will pass over you." Ex.12:13

That lamb was a type of Christ. The Passover lamb pointed forward to the Great Altar of Calvary. There Jesus, like the lamb slain in Egypt to save the firstborn from death, gave His Life by dying on the Cross. The Perfect Lamb of God shed His Own Blood to save not only the firstborn, but everyone in the entire world. 1 Jn.2:2; Jn.3:16

The Passover is a type of Christ! 1 Cor.5:7
**"Christ our Passover is Sacrificed for us:"**
 **Jesus gave His Body and Blood for us**!

The explanation of the following Bible studies:
a. The visual illustration.
b. The type of Christ.
c. How it applies to the believer.

## Seven types of Christ in the Passover Lamb

1. a. The Passover Lamb. Ex.12:1-36
   b. Speaks of the death of Christ our Redeemer.
      Isa.53:7; Jn.1:29,36; 1 Cor.5:6,7; 1 Pet.1:18,19
   c. We have been redeemed through the Blood of Christ.
      Rom.5:9,11.
2. a. A male of the first year (lamb in the very
      prime of its life). Ex.12:5
   b. Speaks of Jesus offered Himself up for Sacrifice for
      our sins in the very Prime of His Life.
   c. We are to serve the Lord without fear, in holiness and
      righteousness all the days of our lives.Lk.1:74,75
3. a. A lamb without Deut.15:21; Lev.22:19-25
   b. Speaks of Jesus God's Perfect Lamb without blemish
      or spot. Lev.22:19,20; Num.19:2; Deut. 15:21;
      Isa.53:6,9; Dan. 9:7, 24; Zech. 9:9, Lk.1:35; 4:34;
      23:14; Jn.18; 8:46; Ac.3:14; 4:27-30;7:52;13:28,35;
      2 Cor.5:21; Heb.1:9; 7:26-28; 4:15; 9:14; 1 Pet.1:19;
      2:22; 3:18; 1 Jn.2:29; 3:3, 5, 7; Rev.3:7.
   c. The Holy Spirit lives within us, and under His
      influence and direction we must strive for perfection.
      To be without blemish or spot. Lk.13:24; Col.1:22;
      Jude 24; Mt.5:48; Heb. 6:1; Eph. 5:27
4. a. The Lamb was set apart four days before the
      Passover to be tested! It was examined before it was
      to be offered for sacrifice. Carefully inspected for no
      defeats: such as blindness, deafness, not crippled, etc.
      Ex.12:5; Deut.15:21; Lev.22:19-25.
   b. Speaks of Jesus set apart. He was tested and
      examined. Jesus proved His holiness.
      Lk.11:53,54; Mk.12:13,14; Jn.8:46.
      Jesus entered Jerusalem in the Triumphal Entry
         exactly four days before the Passover to be crucified.

    c. We are set apart from this present evil world.
Jesus said, we will be examined.
2 Cor.6:14-18; 1 Cor.11:28; Rev.18:3,4
We will be tested. Jn.15:19,20; Mt.10:24,25;
1 Pet.4:12,13.

5. a. The Lamb was slain. Ex.12:6; Lev. 23:5
    b. Speaks of Jesus Crucified. Isa.53; Mt.27:35; Mk.15:24; Lk.23:33; Jn.19:33; 2 Cor.5:21
This shows us of the tremendous sufferings of Jesus In bearing our sins, sorrows and sickness on the altar of His Cross in His Own Body on the Tree.
Jesus, "Endured the cross," Heb.12:2; 13:20 He was made a curse for us and suffered the penalty of hell. A type of the lamb roasted. Jesus died, so that we may live. Jn.12:24
    c. We are innocent through His Blood.
Rom. 6:6 "Knowing this, that our old man is crucified with Him, that the body of sin might be destroyed, that henceforth we should not serve sin."
We are crucified with Christ. Gal. 5:24; 2:20; Rom.12:1,2.

6. a. The Lamb was killed by the whole assembly of the congregation. Ex.12:6.
    b. Speaks of Jesus killed by all of us. Lk.18:31-34
    c. The unsaved kill Christ every day by rejecting Him. The saved kill Him spiritually by disobedience.
Ac.4:27,28
When we willfully sin we put Him to an open shame. Heb. 6:6 We all once killed Jesus, but now the saved are alive in Him. Let's continue to be like Him and to lift Him up continually. Jn.14:20; 15:57.

7. a. Not a bone of the lamb was broken.
Ex.12:46; Num.9:12
Speaks of Jesus, not a bone of Him was broken. The custom was the legs of the crucified one was to be broken so he could not crawl away if he was still alive. When the soldiers came to break the leg of Jesus. He was already dead. This was in specific fulfillment of God's prophecy. Jn.19:33-37
"A bone of Him shall not be broken." Ps.34:20
   b. Speaks of the unbroken strength of Jesus!
Death had no lasting hold on Him: Lk.24:6
" Jesus is not here, but is risen remember how He spoke unto you when He was yet in Galilee."
Jesus is the First-fruits of the Resurrection.
1 Cor.15:20
   c. Death has no hold on the believer.
1 Cor.15:2
"But every man is resurrected in his own order Christ the First-fruits; afterward they that are Christ's at His Coming." When Jesus died upon the Cross of Calvary the veil guarding the way into the Holy of Holies in the Temple (the successor to the Tabernacle) was rent from top to bottom. God and not man tore the Veil in half showing us that now we may enter into the presence of God through the Blood of Christ! Mt.27:50-53; Heb.10:19,20
Because of the pure, holy Sacrifice of Jesus by the shedding of His Blood and Resurrection, we may now enter into the Presence of God.
Heb.10:19,20; 10:12; 1 Tim.2:5
One of the most powerful Scriptures on the unbroken strength of Jesus in death is in Lk.9:27 Jesus said,
"But I tell you of a truth, there be some standing here,

**Six types that the life is in the blood.**

Blood represents Life. Lev. 17:11
"For the life of the flesh is in the blood: and I have given it to you upon the altar to make an atonement for your souls: for it is the blood that makes an atonement for the soul."
The blood of the Passover Lamb is a type of the Blood of Christ. Mt.26:28; Heb 9:22

The power of the Blood of Jesus is seen in:
1. a. The Blood was sprinkled. Heb.11:28
   It was not enough for the blood of the lamb to be shed in order for the blood to become effective. It had to be applied to the doorposts and the lintel. It had to be sprinkled upon the people, the covenant and on every word. Ex.24:8; Heb.9:18,19; 12:24
   In Egypt the blood of the Passover Lamb saved all the first born of Israel from death who applied it. Ex.12:13.
   b. Speaks of the Blood of Jesus sprinkled for us to pass from death unto life. 1 Pet.1:2
   c. It is not enough for us that Jesus shed His blood. We must through faith in His Blood apply it to our hearts if we want to receive the cleansing it provides.
   Rom.3:25; Rev.12:11
   We are saved from spiritual death under the Blood of Christ. When God looks upon us. He sees us through the shed Blood of His Only Begotten Son, and He passes over us! We have escaped death, never to experience it! Rev. 20:6, 14; 2:18.
2. a. The blood was applied to the door. Ex.12:22
   b. The Blood of Jesus applied to our life, speaks of us becoming partakers of His divine nature. 2 Pet.1:4.
   c. It is by faith that we apply the Blood Promises to ourselves. Rom. 3:25; Ex.12:13.

3. a. The blood was put on the lintel and side posts. Ex.12:7,22 The Israelites were not to put the blood at the back of their houses. There is a back way to hell, but no back way to Heaven! We must keep His Blood at the front door and not be ashamed of His Blood!
   b. The blood on the doorpost speaks of open confession of the power of the blood! Speaks of the blood of Christ in our open confession of Him.
   c. The blood upon the door speaks of the Blood of Jesus in and upon our life. In an open confession. We need to openly confess Christ. In Mk. 8:38
   Jesus said, "If we are ashamed of Him here, He will be ashamed of us before His Father in heaven."
   Mt.10:32,33 We must not be ashamed of His Blood upon us!
4. a. The blood was not put on the threshold Ex.12:7
   b. Speaks of reverence for the Blood of Jesus.
   c. We must have reverence for HisBlood. Careful not to trample His Blood under our feet. Heb.10:29
   His Blood is Precious. I Pet.l:19.
5. a. The blood was a means of preservation. The children of Israel were saved from death because the angel of death passed over when he saw the blood. Ex.12:12,13.
   b. Speaks of the Blood of Christ is our means of preservation. The cleansing of our soul and body. I Jn.l:9.
   c. A type of the Blood of Christ keeping us from death and sin as we walk in Him.1 Jn.5:7; Eph. 2:13
   God, sees us through the Blood of His Son. What a glorious message we have for this world! The Blood of Jesus is our preservation. We are kept from the wrath of God, the curse of the law and the damnation of hell! Rom. 8:1.

6. a. The blood of the lamb applied without anything added was a perfect protection from judgment for the nation of Israel. Ex.12:13
   b. Speaks of the Blood of Christ is our perfect protection. Heb.10:10,14
   c. His Blood cleanses us from all sin! The Blood of Jesus itself, with nothing added is enough for our perfect protection. His Blood gives us the victory over sin, death, judgment and everything else the devil will use to accuse us or come against us with, because in the Sacrifice of Christ we have received His Blood Atonement! Rom. 5:9,11
   We overcome all things by the Blood of our Lamb, Jesus Christ and by the word of our testimony! Rev. 12:11

**Three types in the eating of the Passover Lamb.**
1 Cor.5:7,8
1. a. All of the lamb was eaten. Ex.12:10.
   b. Speaks of Jesus the Living Lamb of God is the Living Word! Jn.1:1, 14
   c. God did not intend the Passover lamb to be looked at, but to be fed upon. Israel ate the lamb before they left Egypt. Jesus is in us, then we are saved, and then we leave the world to serve Him! God does not intend for us to admire Jesus for His Sacrifice. God wants us to take Jesus into our lives. Jn.6:53-57
   To feast upon the Living Word. To take all of Jesus within us! The Israelites ate all of the lamb, speaks of Jesus within us! Col. 1:27
   "Christ in you, the hope of glory:" Mt.4:4
   We desire the fullness of His Redemption and blessing, so lets accept the responsibility of service and be faithful! Rev. 2:10.

2. a. The lamb was eaten immediately. Ex.12:10
Speaks of receiving Christ the Lamb. The Word of God, Now! When we hear God's message of eternal life. We should receive and act upon it.
2 Cor.6:2 "(For he saith, I have heard thee in a time accepted, and in the day of salvation have I succoured thee: now is the accepted time; time; behold, now is the day of salvation."
3. a. After the lamb was eaten be ready to leave. Ex.12:11.
The lamb was eaten with loins girded, shoes on, staff n hand, eaten in haste. Israel left Egypt to serve the living God! Ex.12:I I
   b. Speaks of leaving the world, serving and revealing Christ to all! Rev.18:4,5.
   c. We must be ready to proclaim God's Word. To reveal Christ to all.
   2 Tim.4:2; Heb. 3:7; 4:7; Rom. 1:16,17

**The Great Exodus!**
The nation of Israel left Egypt with its slavery, bondage and captivity. Under the blood of the lamb and led by the Cloud of Glory. It was a time for rejoicing!

Under the Precious Blood of Christ, and led by the power of the Holy Spirit we too have made the Great Exodus! 2 Cor.6:14-18; Rev. 18:4,5.

We have made a complete separation from this present evil world. We said good-bye to sin and Satan. We have left this world, the flesh and the devil far behind us! Rom.12:1,2

We have been redeemed with the Precious Blood of Christ as of a Lamb without blemish and without spot. We are standing with our loins girt about with truth, and our feet shod with the preparation of the Gospel of Peace.
Eph. 6:13-20; Jn..8:31-36.

Our message is found in
Heb. 9:12
"Neither by the blood of goats and calves, but by His own blood He entered in once into the holy place (Holy of Holies) having obtained eternal redemption for us." Heb.10:19; 9:8.

**Have you been washed in the Blood of the Lamb, Jesus Christ?**

**The Power of the Blood of Jesus is Seen in His:**
1. **Redeeming Blood.**
   The Passover. Ex.12:13; 1 Pet.1:18,19
2. **Atoning Blood.** The Altar of Sacrifice
   Lev.17:1; Mt.26:28; Heb.9:22; Rom.5:9,11
3. **Cleansing Blood.**
   The leper's. Lev. Ch.13 etc. 1 Jn.1:7.
4. **Sacrificing Blood.**
   In the book of the Covenant every promise is endorsed in blood. Heb.10:29; 13:12
5. **Consecrating Blood.** The priest and the ram of consecration. (The right ear, thumb and great toe) Lev.8:22-24; 1 Cor.6:19
6. **Pleading Blood.**
   The Mercy Seat. Lev.16:14,15; Rom.3:24,25
7. **Sanctifying Blood.**
   The Scapegoat Lev.16:21,22; Heb.13:11,12
8. **Life Giving (Living) Blood.** The Sacrifice.
   Lev. Chs.1-10; Jn.6:54-57

"If we walk in the light, as He is in the light, we have fellowship one with, another and the blood of Jesus Christ His Son cleanses us from all sin." 1 Jn.1:7

The next great event to take place on God's prophetic calendar is the calling home of the Body of believers in Christ.
I Thess.4:13-18; I Cor.15:51-53; Phil.3:20

## Typology Chart

**Typical Colors**
**White, Blue, Purple, Scarlet,**

**Typical Metals**
**Gold**, speaks of His Deity, Divinity.
**Silver**, Redemption.
**Brass**, Suffering.

**Typical Numerals**
**One**, speaks of Unity, Oneness.
   Eph.4:4-6."There is one body, and one Spirit, even as ye are called in one hope of your calling; one Lord, one faith, one baptism, one God and Father of all, who is above all, and through all, and in you all."
   There is a oneness among God's people!
**Two**, Witness and Testimony.
   Rev.3:14. Jesus is, "The Faithful and True Witness,"
   Col.1:15. He is,
   "The Image of the Invisible God, He manifests, makes known the Father!
   Lk.10:1 Jesus sent out His Witnesses,
   'Two and two before His Face into every city and place, whither He Himself would come."
   Heb.10:28; 1 Tim.5:19; 2 Cor.13:1,2; Deut.19:15-21.
**Three**, Divine Completeness, the Godhead.
Col.2:9, "In Jesus dwells all the fullness of the Godhead bodily" Rom. 1:20; I Jn.5:7,8.
Three also speaks of Abundant Testimony.
Full Manifestation in Redemption:

God, the Father planned His Great Plan of Redemption; (Salvation)
God, the Son, the Lord Jesus Christ fulfilled it;
God, the Holy Spirit witnesses to this Redeeming fact in the Scriptures!

Using the number three in the following examples we can see how exhaustive numerals can be!

Three divisions of the Tabernacle:
   1. Outer Court. 2. Holy Place. 3. Holy of Holies.

Three metals used in the construction of the Tabernacle:
   1. Gold. 2. Silver. 3. Brass.

Three colors often mentioned together:
   1. Blue. 2. Purple. 3. Scarlet.

Three entrances to the Tabernacle.
   1. Gate. 2. Curtain Door. 3. Veil.

Three Lights:
   1. The sun in the Outer Court.
   2. The Candlestick in the Holy Place.
   3. The Shekinah Glory in the Holy of Holies.

Three great feasts of the Jews:
   1. Passover. 2. Pentecost. 3. Tabernacles.

Three liquids used in the Tabernacle:
   1. Blood. 2. Water. 3. Oil.

Three types of sacrifices were offered:
   1. - of the herd; bullocks.
   2. - of the flocks; sheep or goats.
   3. - of the fowl; turtledoves or young pigeons.

Three places where the blood was sprinkled:
   1. Brazen Altar. 2. Golden Altar. 3. Mercy Seat.

Three times the river Jordan was divided miraculously:
1. When Israel crossed into Canaan.
2. When Elijah passed over before his translation.
3. When Elisha returned after Elijah's translation.

Jonah was in the belly of the whale for three days and three nights. Jon. 1:17.

Jesus spent three days and nights in the tomb (heart of the earth). Mt.12:40.

The Gospels record three times God spoke from heaven:
1. At the baptism of Jesus. Mt.3:17
2. At His Transfiguration. Mt.17:5
3. Before the Passover. Jn.12:28.

Jesus raised three people from the dead:
1. The daughter of Jarus. Mark 5:22 .
2. The son of the widow of Nain. Lk.7:14
3. Lazarus. Jn.11:43.

Christ was Crucified at the third hour. Mk.15:25 .

His accusation was written in three languages over His Head:
1. Hebrew. 2.Greek. 3. Latin.Lk.23:38; Jn.19:20.

The three-fold nature of man:
1. Spirit. 2. Soul. 3. Body. 1 Thes.5:23; Heb.4:12.

Following are a few types from each catagory that apply to redemption:

**Four**, Yieldingness.

Jn.10:17, 18.

Jesus said,

"My Father loves Me, because I lay down My life, that I might take it again. No man takes it from Me, but I lay it down of Myself. I have power to take it again. This commandant have I received of My Father."

Isa.53:7,8; Mt.26:53.
  Weakness. We live by the power of God.
  2 Cor.13:4
  "Though He was crucified through weakness,
    yet He lives by the power of God.
  For we also are weak in Him, but we shall live
  with Him by the power of God toward you."
**Five**, Grace.
  Jn.1:17.
  "The Law was given by Moses, but grace and truth came
  by Jesus Christ." Rom.3:24 ,29,30; Gal. 3:24
**Seven**, (see Candlestick)
**Eight**, Resurrection.
  The number of New Beginning. After seven days
  have passed. The eighth day begins the new week. Jesus
  arose from the dead on the eighth day. The first day of
  the week. Apart from His Resurrection, there are eight
  other cases of resurrection recorded in the Bible:
  Three in the Old Testament.
      I Kgs.17:17-22; 2 Kgs.4:32-37; 13:20,21
  Three in the Gospels. Mk.5:35- 42; Lk.7:1 1-15;
      Jn.11:1-45
  Two in the book of Acts. Acts 9:36-41; 20:9-12.
**Nine**, Human perfection. Under the influence,
  direction and living by the Holy Spirit.
  9 Beatitudes. Mt. 5:3-11.
  9 Virtues. 2 Pet. 1 :5-7.'
  9 Fold example of Patience. 2 Cor. 6:4,5
  9 fold cluster of the Fruit of the Spirit.Gal. 5:22,23.
  9 Gifts or operations of the Spirit. 1 Cor. 12:8-10.
**Six**, Imperfection.
**Ten**, Perfect Order.

**Twelve**, Governmental Perfection
**Forty**, Testing.

**Typical People**
**Aaron,** Christ, our Great High Priest.
**Moses**, Christ our Deliverer, Ruler and Prophet.
**Bezaleel**, a type of the Spirit-filled believer.
**Aholiab**, a type of Grace.
**Joshua**, Christ our Leader.
**Melchizedek**, Christ our Priest and King.
**Shepherd**, Christ the Good Shepherd.
**Aaron's sons** the ministering priests.
   We are the priesthood of believers.

**Typical Places**
**Egypt**, A type of sin and the world. A place of death and bondage.
**Kadesh-barnea**, Place of decision.
**Promise Land,** Spirit-filled Life or Living.
**Desert,** Temptation or Persecution.
**Sodom and Gomorrah**, Wickedness.
**Wilderness**, purging out the carnality of the Carnal Christian.
**New Jerusalem**, the Celestial City.
**Cities of refuge**, Christ our Protection.
**Rephidim**, refreshing or Life of the Spirit.

**Typical Objects**
**Sword**, Word of God. Eph. 6:17; Heb.4:12; Rev.1:16; 2:12 .
**War**, Spiritual Conflict. Eph. 6:12.

**Key**, Authority or Knowledge.
   Mt.16:19; 18:18 ; Rev.1:18.
**Stone**, Christ the Chief Corner Stone.
   Isa.28:16; 8:14; Rom.9:33; Ac.4:1; Ps.118:22;
   Mt.21:42; Eph.2:20; 1 Pet.2:7, 8
**Stones**, (onyx and precious) A type of Believers.
   Mal.3:17; 1 Pet.2:5
**Wood**, Humanity (Incorruptibility of the Human nature of our Lord Jesus Christ).
   Isa.53:2; Lk.1:35; Mt.1:2
**Sheep**, God's People.

**Typical Events**
**Exodus**, a mass departure. A great going out.
**Wilderness Journey**, Self crucifixion.
**Passover,** Death of Christ.

**Typical Food**
Oil, a type of the Holy Spirit. Christ the anointed.
   Isa.61:1-3; Lk.4:18, 19; Ac.10:38
   The believers anointing. 1 Jn.2:27
**Fish**, speak of men. Mt.4:19; Mk.1:17; Lk.5:10
**Milk**, Food for babes in Christ. 1 Cor.3:1-3; Heb.12:1;
   1 Pet.2:1,2
**Meat**, Food for mature believers.
   Heb.5:12-14; 1 Cor.14:20; Phil.3:15
**Fruit**, Increase or Multiplication.
**Spices**, Christ our Sweet Smelling Savor.
   Eph.5:2; 2 Cor.2:14,15; Lev.1:9; Num.18:17
**Salt**, Incorruptibility or Faithfulness.
   (God's Covenant is called a Covenant of Salt).

Lev.2:13; Num.18:19; 2 Chr.13:5; Col.4:6; Ezek.43:24
**Bread**, Nourish. A means of sustaining life:2 Cor.9:10
**Unleaven bread**, True doctrine. 1 Cor.5:7, 8
**Leaven bread,** false doctrine.
Lk.12:1; Mt.16:6, 11, 12; Mk.8:15; 1 Cor.5:6-8
**Bitter herbs**, Bondage and slavery.

**Typical Animals**
**Lamb / Ram**, Christ, the Perfect Offering.
Jn.1:29, 36; 1 Pet.1:19; Rev.5:6; 13:8; 12:11; Isa.53:7
**Sheep**, God's People.
**Bullock /Oxen**, Strength or Service.
**Lion**, Rulership.
**Birds**, Spirit beings (usually evil).
**Goat**, Sin or the sinner.
**Serpent**, Satan.

**Natural Phenomena**
**Flood**, Judgment.
**Rain**, Blessing.
**Wind**, Might or Power.
**Water**, (great bodies of) Nations).

**Types are not Symbols**.
Symbols are not as close in likeness as types are, but they do hold a high significance. A symbol is that which stands for, reminds us of or represents something else that already exists.

**Symbols applied to Jesus from the four Gospels:**
In Matthew, a lion is the symbol of a King.
   Jesus, is the King of Kings.
In Mark, an ox is the symbol of strength and service.
   Jesus is the Servant who came to Serve.
In Luke, a man is the symbol of mankind.
   Jesus is The Perfect Man.
In John, an eagle is the symbol of Spiritually.
   Jesus is the divine Son of God.

**Symbols**
**Fire**, A symbol of the Presence of God:
   In favor of Ex.3:2; 19:18.
In judgment of, Gen. 19:24;
   Num. 16:34,35; Deut.4:24; Heb. 12:29

**Horns**, symbol of Power.Dan.8:3,4.
**Cross**, symbol of Christianity.
**Dove**, is the symbol of Peace and Purity.

**Symbols applied to the Human Body:**
**Head**, Mind.
**Eye**: Knowledge.
**Ear**, Listening.
**Lips / Mouth**, Testimony.
**Shoulders**: Strength (for burdens)
**Breast**, Affection.
**Heart**, Love.
**Hands**, Service.
**Back**, loins, thighs, Power and Strength.
**Feet**, Walk or Conduct.

**Types are not the same as Prophecy.**
Types are only in a sense a sort of Prophecy.
Prophecy is the for telling of future events.
Gen.49:1; Num.24:14.

Example:
1. **Prophecy that Christ would die as God's Passover Lamb for our sins.** Isa.53:5, 8, 10
   Fulfilled from 500 to 600 years.
   1 Cor.5:7; 15:3, 4; Mt.20:28; 26:28; Rom.6:6, 8; 8:32; 2 Cor.5:21
2. **Christ will die as God's provided Sacrificial Lamb.** Isa.53:5, 6, 10, 12
   Fulfilled 700 years later.
   2 Cor.5:21; 1 Cor.15:3; Rom.5:8
   Also speaking to people for edification and comfort.
   1 Cor.14:3

**There are three kinds of prophecy.**
1. **The gift of prophecy.** Teaching us of what is to Come.
2. **The Spirit of prophecy.**
   Rev.19:10; 1:1,19; 4:1; 7:1,9; 15:5; 18:1; 19:1
   Foretelling future events. Showings things to come.
3. **Fulfilled prophecy.**
   The purpose is Confirmation. Jn.13:19
   All by the same Spirit!

Two fifths of the Bible is prophecy.

All prophecy has already been fulfilled that applies to Redemption, except the redemption of our bodies!

CPSIA information can be obtained at www.ICGtesting.com
Printed in the USA
LVOW070356100512

281139LV00002B/185/A